PROBLEMATICA*

PROBLEMATICA*

* George Murray
Introduction by Adam Sol

ECW

* *New and Selected Poems, 1995–2020*

Published by ECW Press
665 Gerrard Street East
Toronto, Ontario, Canada M4M 1Y2
416-694-3348 / info@ecwpress.com

MISFIT

Editor for the Press: Michael Holmes / a misFit book
Cover design: Rachel Ironstone

LIBRARY AND ARCHIVES CANADA CATALOGUING IN PUBLICATION

Title: Problematica : new and selected poems 1995-2020 / George Murray ; introduction by Adam Sol.

Other titles: Poems. Selections

Names: Murray, George, 1971- author. | Sol, Adam, 1969- writer of introduction.

Identifiers: Canadiana 20210209003

ISBN 978-1-77041-533-1 (HARDCOVER)
ISBN 978-1-77305-773-6 (EPUB)
ISBN 978-1-77305-774-3 (PDF)
ISBN 978-1-77305-775-0 (KINDLE)

Classification: LCC PS8576.U6814 A6 2021 | DDC C811/.6—dc23

We acknowledge the support of the Canada Council for the Arts. Nous remercions le Conseil des arts du Canada de son soutien. This book is funded in part by the Government of Canada. *Ce livre est financé en partie par le gouvernement du Canada.* We acknowledge the support of the Ontario Arts Council (OAC), an agency of the Government of Ontario, which last year funded 1,965 individual artists and 1,152 organizations in 197 communities across Ontario for a total of $51.9 million. We also acknowledge the support of the Government of Ontario through the Ontario Book Publishing Tax Credit, and through Ontario Creates.

ONTARIO CREATES

ONTARIO ARTS COUNCIL
CONSEIL DES ARTS DE L'ONTARIO
an Ontario government agency
un organisme du gouvernement de l'Ontario

Canada Council for the Arts | Conseil des arts du Canada

Canada

PRINTED AND BOUND IN CANADA

PRINTING: FRIESENS 5 4 3 2 1

MIX
Paper from responsible sources
FSC® C016245
FSC www.fsc.org

Books by George Murray

POETRY

Carousel (Exile Editions)
The Cottage Builder's Letter (McClelland & Stewart)
The Hunter (McClelland & Stewart)
The Rush to Here (Nightwood Editions)
Whiteout (ECW Press)
Diversion (ECW Press)
Problematica (ECW Press)

APHORISMS

Glimpse (ECW Press)
Quick (ECW Press)

FOR CHILDREN

Wow Wow and Haw Haw (Breakwater Books)

For Elisabeth

Contents

Introduction to George Murray

George Murray is the first friend I made by writing a book review. Way back in 2003, when the *Globe and Mail* still printed full coverage of single books of poetry, I wrote 500 words on *The Hunter* and soon after met its author. George was appreciative of my praise of the book, forgiving of my quibbles, and demonstrated a gregarious presence much more obsessive and erudite than his self-deprecating persona would imply. We were then part of a crop of poets that was just emerging "on the scene," such as it was. We felt we were poised to inherit something.

Members of that generation of poets have since won major prizes and earned international readerships. Some maintain prominent editorial or teaching positions or have become influential advocates for the arts in their communities. Others have brought harm upon themselves and others. Some have done more than one of these things. We all have our share of stories to tell. But for a group of Gen X slackers, we have done reasonably well.

What I've learned since then is that the feeling of being "poised to inherit something" is the thing you lose as you enter middle age. Whatever that "something" was dissipates or transforms, or perhaps we begin to wonder why we wanted some things in the first place. We have certainly learned in recent years to question why *we* were the ones who seemed "poised to inherit," and who might have been excluded from those feelings for one reason or another.

Yet, whatever equivocations and apologies travel with us, there are also the poems and projects that we cultivated and struggled over and sculpted along the way, and for which we still reserve affection, and maybe an ember of pride. So perhaps it's appropriate that some poets of our generation have begun to publish "New and Selected" collections of poetry, as a way to summarize the beginnings of their careers, to reset and clarify the past, and to look out towards what may come next. These books serve as a record of how we got here, snapshots of early promise and energy, and the steady path through doubt to more complexity, more accomplishment, back to doubt, and around again.

In comedy, the role of the Fool is to make chaos, to generate fun. He can be bawdy, he can be cruel, he can move the plot along or stop it in its tracks. And he always seems to know that he's trapped in a play—he's the one character who can look out at the audience and shrug. He knows the limits of his form, and will push against it, though never until it breaks. It's comedy, after all, and everyone in a comedy deserves a happy ending.

In tragedy, the Fool has more delicate work: she pokes holes in the hero's self-importance, but only as far as his mood will allow. She can still be bawdy, she can still be cruel, but much more of the cruelty is directed at herself. And at the end of the day, the Fool longs for a world where she is the force of chaos, where the jokes are double entendres and not twists of fate. That makes the tragic Fool a kind of moralist, reminding us of better days when princes behaved honourably and the worst that could happen was to be the butt of one of her pranks.

So, when I say there's something of the Fool about George Murray, I'm not just teasing him, though that's an added benefit. Reading over his first two books, *Carousel* and *The Cottage Builder's Letter*, I recall the comic jester in them: the parade of outcasts, charlatans, and tricksters; the boyish cruelty; the wit and pleasure in the clever turn of phrase; the young poet stretching his muscles and developing his craft. An emblematic figure for me is the Egyptian soldier who survives the massacre of his forces in the Red Sea, "swims away from Moses," and is "free to strike out in any direction for land." I love that image of the survivor nearly cleansed of his past and his identity, ready for a new life.

But starting with *The Hunter*, the jester's face paint begins to peel and crack, giving his work a different flavour of searching and desperation. So much more is at stake. It's no accident that this is the book that arrived on the heels of the events of September 11, 2001, when the trajectory of the world seemed to have shifted more towards tragedy. "Does no one else feel it? The pressure? / The unease?" he asks in "Weathervane." There's a sense that the world has broken and the poems are an exploration of that broken-ness, the way a child will shake a silent electric toy to hear the pieces rattling around inside.

This vein of darkness, still tinged with wit and mischief, is what I see as the defining characteristic of George's work until now. George does not build his poems from personal anecdotes—there are precious few biographical details of the kind that some poets make the heart of their work. What we get instead are objects and observations, characters and conjectures, explorations that try to see the world with the off-kilter clarity that it deserves.

Another characteristic of his work is the commitment to form, though the forms he uses are often structures of his own invention. The playfulness and virtuosity that produced all of the sonnet-length variations of elegy in *Carousel* also came up with "thought rhyme" in *The Rush to Here* and upended slogan in *Diversion*—and even in his collections of aphorisms, though they are not contained in this volume. The image I get is of a gem-cutter turning and turning a stone to see all the ways it refracts the light. One has to be a maximalist obsessive to accomplish this. The repeated questions are: is there one more of these I can create? Is there another? And maybe another? What further variations of the form can be revealed? What does the form itself reveal?

So, to sum up: George Murray is an obsessive jester, a connoisseur of phraseology, a lyric explorer, a bitter wit, a tragic rascal. If you are new to his work, this collection is a crash course in that sensibility, full of pleasures, voices, surprises, and questions. If you are already a fan, this is an outstanding way to revisit the best of what George has brought to the poetic conversation to this point, and chart the beginnings of his next trajectory.

One new poem sports the title, "You Can't Say Anything Anymore," which sums up a fair bit of what I'm trying to say about George's work. There's an implicit joke here about our current moment, and fears of saying offensive or inappropriate things in public spaces. The poem refers to dirty laundry in a literal and figurative sense. There may be a worry about how an '80s-era John Cusack movie would hold up under current standards. But the poem, by virtue of its very existence, proves its title wrong. There *are* things that we can still, abashedly, with qualification and context and joking aside, say. His approach may not take itself as seriously as Beckett's "You must go on. I can't go on. I'll go on," but it rejects with similar determination the doubt that haunts us in the churn of our changing world.

George Murray's eye for the uncomfortable, his *Problematica* sensors, have only gotten more keen and nuanced as his red hair has been seasoned with salt. In that sense, he has fulfilled the early promise and energy I saw when I first encountered his work. Here are gathered George's various ways of speaking in poetry, his wit, vision, and complaint defying the silence. I for one am glad to have them here in my hand, and hope you will get as much pleasure from them as I do.

—ADAM SOL

from *Carousel*

Exile Editions
2000

At least I always predicted things would end this way.

THE CARNIE'S OBITUARY

Dead in a Ferris wheel crash at forty-three, he was laid
below an overpass by the highway, clad as he would
have wanted in his best: rattlesnake boots, jeans,
a leather vest, two arms full of green dragon tattoos;
& they had an open casket as the cars whizzed by
above, brought balloons, pink clouds of candy-floss,
sticky pinwheel lollies, shabby brass darts
with bent red flights, a string of flashing marquee bulbs
in patio-lantern covers, an orange tiger on a leash;
& in a moment of silence from the bullhorns, the bells
of the carousel, the speeding traffic, his will was read,
the inheritance handed out: for each a Throwing Ring,
a single chance to toss a winner, to circle his head
in a rubber halo & help him bluff his way into heaven.

THE MEDIUM'S OBSERVANCE

She always predicted she would return
to betray answers to the question of life,
universe, & death *(Be in my studio,*
she said, *three days after I am buried*
& all will be revealed!), yet when
they arrived in droves, the pedals
that shook the table, the switches that lit
her crystals, the strings that levitated
her chair, the bellows that moaned
like lost souls, all lay exposed & in
disrepair; a note on the hollow table
full of bones & wet tea leaves reading,
For some questions, any answer is good
enough. (Twenty-five dollars, please.)

THE AERIALIST'S FALL

For years she hung from a slim thread performing
amazing feats of contortion in the air, her silver
        suit flashing in & around the trapeze, suspended
        from fingers, knees, elbows, toes, feet, wrists,
chin, teeth, any part of her body with bones
able to lock into a hook; but at forty she fell

        pregnant, was replaced by younger, slimmer girls
        who wore less clothing, more makeup, had gold
dust in their hair; & though these girls talked her out
of abortion, it was they who stood by, awestruck
        at her skill as she clung to life in the hospital bed,
        twisting through the pain: the breech working
as gravity to bring her down & the intermittent line
of the EKG the unravelling cord to which she clung.

THE LION TAMER'S EMBALMING

Some called him *totemic* (a tamer with a bit of the lion
in him), others a *saprophyte*; yet regardless, you can all
guess how he went, & it wasn't pretty, neither the act
nor the conundrum of burial: his half-corpse forcing us
to kill the beast, spill its belly in the Three Ring dirt
to retrieve the missing pieces needed to finish the puzzle
(sad, he had been so proud of being a simple man in life);
but what came pouring out looked largely uniform,
the bloody pre-performance feed suddenly so similar
to the man himself (a mess of blue digestive juices),
so, we voted to defer the decision & bury them together,
send them on as a *symbiote*: the lion & the tamer,
each with a bit of the other inside, trust that whoever received
them was more suited than we to judge what belonged to whom.

THE VENTRILOQUIST'S HOMICIDE

His agent was cleared as a suspect when they discovered there
hadn't been contact in years: the work drying up as the puppet boom
ended with the decade, the jibes from Jimmy Rebb, his favourite
dummy (*Knee Figure, please*) now just insults that seemed
to go nowhere, to become more & more elliptical (*Inside jokes
with no one inside*); but a subpoenaed therapist cleared up
the confusion (*As they seem to do*), jesting (*From the side of his mouth,
of course*) that ventriloquism is perhaps the only vocation
that willfully cultivates multiple personalities, & our man
(*Out of work*) was forced to sell his figures to eat, causing a case
of overcrowding (*A state of mental Darwinism*): one character
choking at the others for rights to the only mouth, until all that was
left was a corpse hanging from the rafters in the basement,
good old Jimmy Rebb crumpled (*Like a broken spine*) at its feet.

THE DIVINER'S EULOGY

Without the children of which she always
dreamed the arrangements were left
in the hands of friends, a committee who,
to their utter horror, were forced to cremate
her remains three days after her death;
A tragic violation, some cried, *a travesty*
of karma; Only a circumstance, others implied,
of fate, of chance, or perhaps a simple
testament to the nature of skill: each hole
dug since her final breath filling slowly
with black water, its gurgling, so dear
to her in life, now hindering a final peace;
her pelvis tilting like a rod above each
potential grave as though bearing down hard.

THE ASTROLOGER'S LAST TESTAMENT

In the later years she was confined to a bed with milky
cataracts that kept from her the brief alignments
night made, the sky spinning from glyphic specks
to a black beach: *The stars are an engine,* she said once,
So, I feel now what I can't see; & true to her word,
she continued to read the dark like Braille, bringing
believers to her side, people who held her bent fingers
at the knuckles as though waiting for the hands to open,
spill like an hourglass the answers to every little
question: *Yellow; She loves you; Yes; Tuesday; Six; A girl;*
Florence; Under the breadbox; yet in that windowless
room full of the faithful, even she was seen to pass,
gasping as she faded: *These are not my stars!* her eyes
shifting below the white as though searching the sky.

THE EXORCIST'S EPITAPH

Beneath his white collar lay the aged
fury with doctrine that effected his death,
for he believed that how souls are damaged
(some unwound as poor fabric, others wreathed
in heavy stitch) is inconsequential.
Evils, he said, *whether exposed as demons*
or dark fathers, exist more as denials
that defy prayers, waters cast, sermons;

further still, the forms these spirits devise
(eyes spindled back, fingers clawed for succour,
shrouded hands steepled) are simply disguises,
appeals for amnesty, answer, candour.
But all failures pass, as did he: in blood,
teeth, & raging eyes that spun with ire (like God's).

THE ESCHATOLOGIST'S END

After being diagnosed with the virus near century's end,
he spent almost twelve frustrated years seeking
proper explanations: reading the Quran, Nostradamus,
the Bible, Mason lore, the Torah, Mayan & Aztec
calendars, the *Sunday Times*, Druidic runes, Buddhist
texts on monastery walls, yearly reports from Dow
Chemical, Pythagorean numerology; & as the end
drew nigh, his gloomy predictions were echoed
by others: the world, they agreed, would soon conclude;
but unlike his embarrassed colleagues, he didn't get
past the stroke of midnight, the clock clicking over
as he fell to complicated pneumonia, a last passage
from his survival journal reading:

My only consolation is
at least I always predicated things would end this way.

THE NUMEROLOGIST'S OBITUARY

Sullying Quantum Physics at Harvard caused, at first,
no real uproar; but two years later, while studying maths
at Trinity College, he was spotted down in
the quadrangle with a stack of occult texts: black covers
pressed with spurious prime numbers & red pentagrams;
& his stolid professors found themselves at sixes
& sevens over the blasphemy, their yearly meet
in October rocked by calls for exile from even
his oldest supporters, the German Physicists: *Nein!*
they exclaimed. *This calculated decadence must cease!*
& though expelled that morning during elevenses tea,
he seemed quite himself by noon; yet later that night

word spread of his jump from a floor that didn't exist.

THE ORACLE'S WILL

Why has it been only the stupid ones with erratic fates
who have come seeking answers? those who burdened me
not with what I could tell, but with what I could not:
edges of truth that, unlike a butterfly's wing, can cause future
currents to shift—don't wander even familiar lands under
a new moon, always bring a friend to an outdoor loo,
fire escapes are for escaping fire, you can't fly, stay indoors
when it rains, it would be prudent to rid yourself of that
corkscrew before she comes over, metal buckles are a bad
idea on this unpredictable lake—loose answers that could
alter the weather time bred long ago; below, my daughters,
I enclose a list of statements as your inheritance:
what couldn't be included is my apology that since your birth
it's always been too soon to tell you it was always too late for me.

. . . & here I digress from the words he has written to tell you
of how my kayak skims the lake, even in the driest years when
the lily pads lose their leaves to low water, the sound below
like the hush of wet sand displaced by a paddle from the beach,
even the quietest strokes passing off as waves on the shore
where the rocks are live with spiders, blackflies, & lined
ghosts of water resting like damp rings in the bowels of trees
where squirrels cling, red heads pointed down at the flat,
worn stone of the north, its peaks & overhangs dark, drawing
me to glide in their shade for long moments, waiting out
the urge to move;
yet I must defer to others: his wife, children,
friends; for while we all suffer when a solipsist dies, it is
these folk who have spent their lives trapped behind his eyes
& are only now beginning to take their first breaths of air . . .

THE PORNOPHILE'S EULOGY

Do we then celebrate the undeniable irony
that it is now he who is being laid roughly
down in the dirt, this surveyor of filth,
his gaunt body naked, wreathed in salmon satin
& involuntarily stiff, bony cheeks hung
with blush, thin lips painted to please, black
hairs & ugly yellow nails still seeming to creep
in from under the skin; or do we smile,
deducing that after years spent accustoming
his ears to the noise of sex, it must be silence
which he finally found erotic: the grave's dark
loam combining a lifetime of little deaths
into one great ecstatic moment where he could
finally come, & go, all at the same time.

THE SOMNAMBULIST'S BURIAL

At the funeral everyone kept expecting him
to rise, to jump out of the coffin
& traipse about the room, use his glassy,
dead eyes to wink at the frightened
minister & read passages from the Bible
he could now personally discredit;

but instead they just buried him,
upright as was his wont, left a bell
to ring in case of false alarm, in case
this great traveller of sleep found
something different down there
in the darkness of the soil, something
that might turn him up and out of his rest
& set him to walking urgently from the bed.

THE NARCISSIST'S KADDISH

By this hillock he lies, for like others
in self-love, he drowned in the idea
of life's impermanence: husband, father,
brother, son, in every role a piece
of himself that would live on in memory,
Yahrzeit & blood, yet he knew that one
day even this would end: his hazel eyes
& dark hair losing to the final dooms
of death & birth like mountains turned to hills
under water & wind; so for shivah
we cover the mirrors & say farewell,
praying that while these carved words may one
day fade, they will never be indistinguishable
from the beautiful face of stone

THE CORONER'S AUTOPSY

Found in a pool of blood below the examination table,
murder was ruled out when his colleagues opened him
like a doctor's bag:
                                        a loud snap with a sterile jack
to the solar plexus, gloved hands reaching into
the black cavity, the ribs raising on either side
like a crackling drawbridge, pulled up to reveal
the surprising cause of death: exsanguination,
an evacuation of blood from the body as though
the heart gave one great pump, sent every drop of him
out the mouth, ears, nose, eyes, anus, urethra;
no foul play, just the natural holes with which
he was born rebelling in a sudden, overwhelming
case of the willies; a much-needed release after
years of casual judgment in the presence of death.

THE MNEMONIST'S EULOGY

For forty years he secluded himself to work on his theory
that over the course of a lifetime the average person lives
only sixty days, existing solely in *Moments of Being*,
fragments of memory strung together with a loose through-
line called *Self*: a blanket, a favourite toy, a fort, a kiss
on the brow, a scene through a car window, a sibling's body
on a slab, a wedding dress, a particularly deep sigh or two,
an orgasm below the tongue; each moment just a shred
of day but not the day itself, not the dishes, the showers,
the shits, the touching, scratching, driving, stairs, & breaths;
Everything, he wrote in his journal, *we are unsure*
of in mind, heart, & spirit, we reinvent as living; so, as we
gather today to disprove life like he did, let us now take
him into our minds as he lies here, in this moment & no other.

THE CARDIOLOGIST'S ARREST

The report said they found her kneeling
in the warm August sea, a still human
heart cupped to her chest like a handful
of sand; her husband, the late doctor, lying
bare, empty from neck to navel in the town
morgue (having died only hours before
of a massive coronary seizure);
As search lights swung through, the poetic
policeman wrote, *she looked back over*
her shoulder with the flush of an escapee,
& uncupping her hands, let the quiet
muscle float into the shallows where,
in the ancient sanguine mix of salt & water,
it began to beat & swam away.

from

The Cottage Builder's Letter

McClelland & Stewart
2001

O, but please tell us that the art said it all . . .

THE LAST OF THE SINNERS WAITS ON A ROCK FOR NOAH

I stood with the calm of a hunting stork,
the patience of a scarecrow: arms outstretched
for balance, one foot drowned to the ankle
in the floodwaters, the other tucked
inside a knee, one sole gripping my leg,
the other palming like a fist that highest peak.

I lost count at forty days, but still know this—
by twenty the water had chased us up here,
by thirty the heads of my people had sunk below
the rain, by forty memory deserted me
to the awareness I was now all body: bones
and skin waterlogged and salted into this pose.

Around me at times birds flew: sparrow,
split-tailed swallow, nightingale and thrush,
each winging on its last breath
then spinning down into the sea—
never one with a moment's thought given to
saving itself on an arm where blood still flowed.

Sometime recently, I couldn't say when,
a strong but, later I learned, unfaithful crow
came gliding just above the hushed surface—
its cry petulant, as though tired of carrying
the sky: those ailerons, suited to soaring,
camouflaging it like a thief against the Black Sea.

And in its flight, so curiously near, I caught
sight of a dark eye as it closed the distance
to pluck and eat from my hair a twig and leaf,
another determined refugee of the water,
perhaps an only remaining relative,
and in that gleaming oculus I was revealed—

salt flats like a teary desert of old riverbeds
stretching back from my eyes, cracked
white tide rills running like fossilized evidence
of earthly trauma across my lips,
a bleached crown of black hair standing
from my head, withered and hardened.

And, as I started in fright at the face
of a stranger, the fickle crow flew off, unfed,
its wings disappearing over the horizon,
and I was alone again, for a time, until
a seemingly tame rock dove swept in, lighting
on the taut and burnt muscles of an arm—

its slim, peaked body heaving with just
enough breath to keep alive the twitching
of its head, and it stayed a moment
preening and warbling, rummaging for food
among the jetsam of my beard: only
relief, good intentions and hunger in its eyes.

But in its fearless fetching of leaf and branch,
the balance I had for so many days struck
between me, the mountain and the sea
was broken: and slowly, with a creak in
the bones like a keel in a storm,
I began to tip.

In the apology of its stare, also reflecting
both myself and the blue-on-blue horizon,
another scene played before it too fled—
widening eyes, a scorched head tilting away,
the skyline listing to an angle viewed
most often by the awakening and the dead.

THE COTTAGE BUILDER'S LETTER
(Muskoka, 1903)

I.

There are things behind as well

like the nothing he can't think of telling just yet;
he hasn't written a letter in so long
and there's no telling where it might go—

like the blocked runnel road; the late afternoon sun
behind a line of boxcars stalled north to south
on the track, a row of homes with open doors—

like autumn; it was summer when he left,
and he touches a last dazed yellowjacket drunk
on the chill, its sting fallen into his ink pot—

like the peach-blush twilight south and west,
a skin of light over the collapsed barns and homes
on rural routes; the moon tipping in—

like a night where trees and people at the roadside
become dark, armless windmills,
the gears inside turning soundlessly—

like solid rock pushing up between the trees,
moss and scree; space for a cabin or shooting stars,
every streak of light passing behind him—

like the man who plucked him, fresh off the boat
at lakeside, hungry but still able
to swing a hammer; a fist full of broken knuckles—

(There has never been a moon so thin;
such an abundance of everything to build on
                                        but this)

like a knock on the door whose frame isn't built,
a hand on the knob that is only a thought,
a folding knife or a pen opened in a shallow pocket.

II.

Before the work begins there is too much to think of

like the two other men also arrived who have written
long letters home to sisters, children, wives—

like the mistake of leaving the steady gruel of the boat
to pretend anywhere his shadow cast was home—

like shouts from the drunk architect planting stakes
in the soil, painting glyphs on trees and rock—

like the wait for workers to arrive that stretches
into weeks; the food dwindling to apples and berries—

like a thought of sisters left searching for husbands
on the streets of Belfast; any man with pennies enough—

like the hope that sometime before the wood arrives
there will come to him words that will not defy pen—

like seven midnights with stars blocked by clouds;
a growing hunger and worry like childhood—

like a change of month; another week that passes
without a word sent home or sight of a single nail—

like age ten, stealing from the collection plate at church:
ha'penny in from the fingers, penny out in the knuckles—

(the islands dry out, the bay-waters lower; the architect,
cursing the dry summer,

knows the boats can't pass, sets them to hunting;
        but no one is yet so hungry as they were)

like fearing that when finally able to lie down, the letters,
like food and men, might go, or come from, nowhere.

III.

What is brought to him he remakes with his eyes

like the local steamer hauling wood from the mills down river
through the blocked shoals, black smoke as though from a pipe cast
overhead, and rafted in from there; the wet wood a silent passenger,
its knotted mind on those it knew and what it would say if it could—

like the crates of black spikes, the boxes of spruce-handled saws
and hammers wrapped in oilcloth, the hand-mixed mortar;
the corn-dough a hired black cook bakes into travel bread, the raw
onions to feed the Russian mason and the woolly carpenter—

like the letters the Jewish boy brings to him for spelling, every other
word sounded out between them; apple; the thick dark script
of the charcoal blurred by his three-fingered left hand passing over
what is written, paper smoky as lantern glass where unfinished—

like the American woodcutter that arrives by raft from the mill,
chopping for food: a recession making axemen too costly to pay;
the cedar frame for a window sill brought in scattered pieces yet
still standing out like a face hidden amid the planks and timber—

(would that he were a painter or some other skilled in light and were
able to tell each item for what it was;
                                        yesterday, ten words pooled
in his head but hunger and the night drove them off unpenned)

like the fat fox-snake speared with a nail on a long stick, thrashing
in the wet fecund air, its own sharp stink, and the sour smell of men;
held over the fire and made ash, the dark tunnel of its skin
fallen in to become the lead of a pencil held at the ready arm's end.

IV.

Up the hill they move from the wood-raft

like thoughts pressed down into his mind by the planks;
each step a struggle in the wind-scarred rock—

like the merciless red ants that run in the tide rills
of the rock; their throbbing little lives—

like the running water far behind the site lined up
at a beaver dam to pass into the interior lake; but held—

like the muskrat who lies on its back cracking open
mussel shells; inside each only a pearl of flesh—

like the heavy clouds that after the first day
block the sky; the lake only able to mirror stillness—

like the mouth of rocks on the long island seething
with slim garter snakes; one thick rattler waiting outside—

like the month that passes by, from new moon to new
moon, without a shred of blue sky; yet dry as sand—

like the water lilies, flowerless, their stems stretching
inches out of the low water to suspended pads; roofs—

like the smoke of mosquitoes and blackflies that blinds him
from the plan; dry air and time beginning to kill them off—

(he can feel it as he hauls up the last of the supplies;
the waiting)

like the first rain in weeks hitting the pale grey stone;
each drop spreading the deepest Indian indigo—

like the night before the work begins; the silence of sky
torn open for a moment to the last, or first scrap of moon.

v.

Rain ready in the clouds

like a child-laden belly, the mother stooped
in a birthing squat right there amid the blighted
potatoes; seven-year-old girls helping her sit,
an absent husband drunk to six months from dead—

like the men now assembled, waiting for light,
for any signal to begin building;
the evening fire a ring of laughter that works
as well as any walls against the black woods—

like the answers to questions after weeks
of wondering: how trees can grow on the oldest
stones, where men made homes here
without the tradition of ruin—

like yesterday's encounter with the black bear,
its deep huff in the woods a few feet off
as he made water near a shelf of rock; the wet
sound of its feeding, the sharp scent of its departure—

like the thought that tomorrow at least something
will happen; that, even as the stars turn behind
the dark clouds, so much time having been lost,
they are at the nail; the sound of birds—

(he put his hand on a tree, almost thought he felt
a pulse; the air thick as though
                                        from a slow leak of steam)

like the blue moss and lichen rolled in long strips
from the rock, the digging bear having taken the grubs,

but left a new world of earth exposed to the sun;
wind, drops of rain and the seeds from above.

VI.

Between the hammer and the nail there is air

like the memory of an arched door near Tara, a bolt-hole
through which he ran as a child; famine a knotted fist,
a heavy riveting glove, a lump of molten metal in his stomach—

like the memory of fleeing his apprenticeship, the black forges
steaming in massive teakettle bursts; his mother's drawn face
counting pennies, his father's tiny marker grown over with grass—

like the memory of leaves dying near the furnaces
of Liverpool; a crisp brown halo, an aura around
the green, so unlike the ruddy apple turning seen here—

like the memory of the long boat, the heat of the boiler room,
the hammock thickly polluted by hundreds of other bodies;
looking into daylight after weeks under a dark metal sky—

like a memory of first days in this country, sleeping
in fields, under porch stoops, in missions and caves;
the stony sound of water or the watery sound of stone—

like the memory of switching from steel to wood, pipe-fitting,
drilling, the heat of steam through metal left behind; bending
his mind on anything, even wood, better than starving in Ireland—

(there is finally a moment of no thought before his hand begins
to descend, the torque creating a vacuum—
                                        everything he ever wanted pulled in)

like a clear memory of his own unscarred, childhood hands
held out before him, the skin unbroken and unlined, the knuckles
bending without pain or resistance; good tools kept poorly.

VII.

Everything about is not the cottage

like the thoughts he has been chewing for weeks, mulling in
the corners of his teeth as tobacco leaves, worrying
with his tongue; speaking not an option and it is too wet to write—

like the bear, the potential for spring in its hunting crouch,
muscle on muscle sliding under a hidden skin as it stares
into the rain-pocked lake; what reflection there is distorted—

like the hand-cut planks laid in staggered piles
next to live towers of pine; a saw, not forgotten but rusting
near one end, stuck on angle like an axe—

like the soft mounds of wood-dust coloured light as owl-down,
sand or the inside mount of an acorn cap tipped and rolled up
as though fallen off in rest; a worker's bed now mud wet—

like the crested ducks bobbing quietly offshore, the colour
of leather, the colour of sun on the rocks, the colour of dark
shapeless openings in the hillside; mouths with clusters of teeth—

like the rain, almost alive, coming in hard sheets of warm water
as though to clean the dead; the stone made treacherous,
porous, streaming like sweat on brows and cheeks—

like the lull when the clouds seem to be higher, a tower
now just bored to death of rain;

(the words have lost their taste
and the spit is vile and black; there will be weather for letters
tomorrow)

like how in the silence, before the air can recover, the first axes hit the stone ringing, or the first axes hit the ringing stone.

QUESTIONS FOR AN ELDERLY GENTLEMAN

What is this genealogy you have laid down on the sidewalk
like fossilized finch skeletons from some string of islands?

and how many squirrels do you think die of old age, falling from
the branches and hitting the ground with nut-choked cheeks?

and other than the scent of fruit, of livestock, of her hair held up
in loose braids with silk knots, can you remember home?

and in the navy, do you think they really only guessed direction
by the strips of sun and wind that lay across the deck?

and was it just in time for Halloween, the year you realized
the world was ugly: hunchbacks shuffling through the leaves?

and have you been here before, perhaps recently, and it has just
slipped your mind like a name on the tongue?

and when your wife withers, shaking in a chair, your hand on her
fluttering breastbone, how do you keep living a myth made for two?

and do you feel that getting lost here has been at all similar to
the moment of surprise and regret a bird must feel hitting a window?

and is there any point in noticing that some leaves cling longer
to the tree than others; that some apples fall in January?

and if your pictures of her could speak, what could they possibly
add to a thousand words?

and when you first saw the sea, did it look to you like a hem
for the wide skirt of sky or was it a darker day?

and tell me: will all conversation, even between the stupid and
the bored, deepen when there is really nothing left to say?

and what must it be like in a family plagued with cancer, when
tumours bloom more often than children and grow twice as fast?

and have you ever eaten a winter cherry when the pit is frozen,
the flesh so black it is easily disrobed with your tongue and palate?

and do you recognize this house? or this one? or this?

THE TRAIN

From the country I take the train,
a seat against the direction
of travel—
the roadside slipping by
slowly at first,
green at first,
then blurred and grey.

The birds flying towards me
are pulled away into the distance.

I slide into each city
as if leaving—
the familiar landscape
running away from me
and everything new creeping
up behind.

NOSTALGIA FOR THE SECOND JUST PAST

Do you remember how we wore our hair—
look at the way it fell, those silly locks
much thicker or thinner than now, more coloured,
more spiked, more quaffed, or less—
our beards trimmer, longer, heavier
or not covering much of the face, and they still
hadn't grown shaggy quite yet, or they had,
or they were perhaps not even there at all.

And those awful clothes, can you recall who
might have thought of pants like that,
of those colours for shirts, of how collars hung,
weren't present, of the priest-look,
the pauper-look, the academic with patches—
that we did not see how anachronistic,
how foppish, how military we appeared
is only a witness to the immaturity of our day.

Diversion, what there was of it, its abundance,
was that of a simpler time, more intense,
slapstick, tragedy, romance, ironic reference—
how did these things entertain us, enrage us,
so grainy and false, so true we shook our heads
and held our bellies, pounded fists in anger—
those brilliant, stilted, subtle actors working
with our empirical, absurd, jaded minds.
Those homes, what were we thinking—

form over function, function directing form,
the mess of vertical, horizontal space,
architectures of boredom, cladding for the eye,
did we have no shame when we first thought
to decorate, did we have no taste—

everything so monumental, disposable,
a testament to the ages crumbling around us.

And politics, gentle beast, who could have predicted
the surge of fascism, democracy, lazy communism,
of the environmental vote, or an anti-male movement—
we were savage, enlightened, the envy
of every limping nation, a laughingstock
to the world, a beacon, an example, blind mindless
followers, automatons and anarchists, the breath
of all ideas made real by touch of cold.

O, but please tell us that the Art said it all,
said nothing with purpose, without meaning,
is a record, an archive, the simplest of lists—
tell us it said what we were saying with
the permanence of paper, canvas, stone, so we
can at least be satisfied where we are, if not
where we've been, and for once in the history
of our species, live somewhat unashamed.

EXCERPTS FROM GREAT LITERATURES OF THE PAST

I suddenly can't remember the text—
did Mary hold Jesus to her breast
to feed? Was she bare to the waist in public?

And was Félicité the name of the maid
in *Madame Bovary*, the one who stole sugar
from the sideboard and ate it alone in her bed?

And what was the deal with Chiron, that bit about
the poison arrow striking his centaur hide
and sending him into a flight of constellation?

O Sagittarius! O Nostradamus! O Census!
Where are my predictions?
I was promised a few things in the '70s

and have yet to receive them—
I can only remember what I myself have written,
like a youngster with his first publication,

flipping past all the good pieces to find his own.
Was it the Germans who were the bad guys?
The Koreans? The Iraqis? The Canadians?

Did Abraham actually kill his own son
or did he, Isaac, and Ishmael
go on to build the Kaaba at Mecca?

This I know: that little poor girl, Oliver Twist,
she just wanted a wee bit more food—
and the man who wrote her suffering and denial

now hangs upside down with the Devil,
turning as though he were a goose on a spit.

LIBRARY

Maybe you know how
to live in a way
that isn't just about breathing,
but I don't—
so please: reserve this
space for me.

(Rest here a moment
without thinking)

In what manner you choose
to keep your books:
I know this little part of you,
hold it sacred—
it's your other secrets,
if any, that are not safe with me.

DESPITE THE HUNGER AND DELICIOUS TASTE

Despite the hunger and delicious taste of it,
knowledge frightens me—
I don't want to know how lightning works,
or gravity, or the speech-dance of bees.
Cuneiform markings on clay tablets should,
in my opinion, have stayed unreadable—
there would still be wonder, no disappointment
in the boredom between farmers.
I want to live without an awareness
that day and night are simultaneous,
without the ability to reach the white beaches
of Greece on a day's notice,
without the surety that thoughts are not
created and housed in my heart.
I want to believe that a cold spread of fear
that feels like déjà vu is déjà vu,
that when cats stare and hiss at nothing
they are actually confronting something,
that the red and purple spots left floating after
staring into a light are visions.
Is there no recourse for the simple soul
who won't let himself think in allegory—
the impregnation of women by the sun,
the healing properties of musical instruments,
that the sea was once stirred to procreate
by the consumption of severed testicles?
What I'd give to exist
in a state of perpetual ignorance
of things like the distance between stars,
perhaps hundreds of miles above—
or to live thinking the moon has a first name
and children, that they fall in the rain
to be raised by her lover, the sea—

that sometimes when she touches the hills
in the distance someone is crushed—
or that a companion sits there,
some ancient shepherd or dirty satyr
waiting to greet her, to help ease her
creaking bones down into a wide bed of earth.

RAIN

the winemaker's rain falls like fat green grapes
the horse's rain advances in pellets of oats on the field
the student's rain is a hail of red erasers at lunchtime
the father's rain comes and goes
the stone's rain sounds of
the wind's rain introduced angles to the world
the banker's rain dents cars in a barrage of coins
the runner's rain gets pounded underfoot
the pilot's rain begins in a sky that never falls
the tree's rain bends under force from the wind
the moon's rain dots the I of creation
the photographer's rain is slanted lines of solid water
the writer's rain sounds of typewriter strikes
the teacher's rain hangs suspended like coloured chalk dust
the singer's rain runs up from the throat and passes the lips
the traveller's rain falls all over the planet
the astronaut's rain will arrive from the stars
the canine's rain is a hail of yellow fangs in the mouth
the mason's rain flies from under the hammer
the baby's rain rattles from the mobile clouds
the chickadee's rain is a sudden burst of feathers
the illusionist's rain has dis/covered/membered/appeared
the mother's rain holds long inside her
the priest's rain may or may not be there
the reporter's rain has caused much damage
the farmer's rain is family invited to dinner
the marshal's rain always gets its man
the river's rain is a sleet of new children hungry for movement
the wind's rain introduced angles to the world
the rose's rain beats petals into thorns
the miser's rain gets hoarded in bell jars
the artist's rain is slick blue on the canvas
the engineer's rain makes much sense for the planet

the pistol's rain travels straight through the heart
the sister's rain is hand–me–downs from the brother
the brother's rain glosses the eyes of the sister
the feline's rain is indifferent to those it falls on
the lord's rain is the oldest of weapons
the fat man's rain hangs guiltily at the back of the tongue
the enemy's rain chambers itself in the gun
the mayor's rain is short-lived and perfunctory
the television's rain falls in a hundred different channels
the radio's rain requires too much effort
the star's rain raises Braille from the night
the worm's rain pulls itself from the ground
the puddle's rain is the beginning of all clouds
the cloud's rain tears from the end of a thousand faces
the weeper's rain is cousin to the darkest sky
the wind's rain introduced angles to the world
the planet's rain falls less in expectance of more destruction
the hermit's rain holds itself for the day he steps from the cave
the dancer's rain curls drop around drop as it leaps to the earth
the sun's rain is half a rainbow circling the eye
the prophet's rain is the beginning
the philosopher's rain is the middle
the scientist's rain is the end

AN EGYPTIAN SOLDIER ON THE RED SEA SWIMS AWAY FROM MOSES

Even before the swells began to crash back in
I had a bad feeling about the situation, but under orders,
persisted as any good soldier would: pressed on

regardless of the high walls of black water groaning
and straining as though against the side of an invisible
but poorly constructed dike. So far ahead

we could never have caught them anyway, the excited
roar of the Jews, scrambling out of the trench
of sea, tipped off some engineers' instinct

in my mind and I began to divest myself of metal—
first my sword, then my shield, then bronze pauldrons
and the ringing helm of solid copper on my head,

even the gold trappings about my ears and waist
falling surreptitiously from the back of the chariot
and down to the ocean floor where they may,

for all I know, still rest to this day among the skeletons
and fish: rotting to a coral green in the salt of that angry
and insulted tide. While the callings

my people have embraced range from fishwife
to concubine, potter to soldier, farmer to Pharaoh—
every soul raised in the Delta, Egyptian or Jew,

knows the particulars of flooding: it starts with
starry signs that pock the pupil of sky, a fetid thickness
of air, a deep humming of insects,

the numeric significance of water growing as it trickles
through the dampening night. And, yes, while
at every phase of my denuding I mourned the loss

of my family's fortune, honour and luck—
as the bound sea collapsed, its halves of water
rushing together like a majestic clap of hands or

siblings long apart, I was given a vision and embraced
my new position under the sun: that of prognosticator,
diviner, augur of water to cleanse the land—

the only Egyptian naked enough before the fist
of the Jewish god, the only one unidentifiable
in the roiling waves, the only one enough disguised

as human to be left floating, alive, head bare
under the burning Eye of Re—
tattooed arms free to strike out in any direction for land.

from
The Hunter

McClelland & Stewart
2003

Hell, he says, is yet ravenous and it won't be full until you get there.

HUNTER

The forest lies quiet immediately before the axe,
the desert gives up accelerating the wind.

Across the earth game birds and salmon go still,
deer and bison and hoary goats freeze instantly.

It is he who stepped on a lizard's throat and called it
a dragon, he who defeated a mountain village

and named it a kingdom, he who hung for a night
and bled song from his wounds, he who chases

the chariot sun across the sky and never catches it.
Let us retreat to a time of less and more sin, he says,

let us entreat our wives and sisters to birth monsters.
Let us return to the roots of our earliest prophecies.

As a fisherman he has cast his line over and again into
the sea, coming away with only Gilgamesh, Jonah,

Grendel. As a farmer he has set countless seeds
and nuts into runnels of earth and has only managed

to grow Nefertiti, Helen, Guinevere. As a hunter
his knife has run between the ribs of countless ermines,

grizzlies, and blue foxes, yet has never spilled
a drop of blood that wasn't that of Pythagoras,

Ptolemy, Copernicus. He is a man who would tip
the earth, sip from the edge of a continent

as though the seabed were the bowl of a goblet.
Reincarnation, he tells us when we beg,

was removed from the list of reasons not to kill
when we reached the point of more people

alive on the planet than have ever lived
and died in all of history and story. He moves

among us on his beasts, he travels the boar-runs
of the forest without the slightest snap

of twig or branch, he walks across the waters
of our moats and seas, slides between the cracks

in our windowsills, lifts the sheets of our beds,
climbs our bodies to the throat

and lets loose springs of life to course down
the topography of our testament to living.

It is he who stands squinting into the blowing dust
and sand as though tired after a long chase,

he who looks upon us fondly as though
recently given over to love after years spent

in doubt, he who raises the standard
that bears an emblem none of us expected.

For consolation he tells of the buzzard
that has lit on his shoulder where a falcon should,

how he's forced to remind it constantly
with a mailed fist that he is still alive, if just

barely. *In this world*, he says, *everything will be*
claimed by the sand. In this world we are

always wandering the desert. In this world the desert
is the Promised Land. In this world the Promised Land

is still just over the horizon. In this world, he says,
drawing a blue blade with a shriek that runs shivers

up and down the mountain sides,
the horizon is what you see when you look up.

WEATHERVANE

The weather has suddenly become inarticulate,
unable to confess its own crimes,
much less finger those who abused it.

It is time to parent the monsters of this world,
time to police the rabbits and hamsters, it is time
to execute the innocents in ingenious machines.

Does no one else feel it? The pressure?
The unease? There have been predictions
of a whole lot of an unspecified something

for quite some time. The continents
are as moody as a life-raft lost deep at sea,
the passengers as excited and hopeless as well.

During the good weather a wasp gets caught between
the panes of a window; everyone in the room
is safe from its sting, but still uncomfortable.

Perhaps, as the wasp looks for a way out
of a trap that was never set and cannot be seen,
they can't help concluding

things are going undone, purposes unfulfilled.
If life keeps getting better, then it should always
be the best (or so logic dictates), but nothing

is so memorable it can't be forgotten.
In the worst weather, while God ignored
Noah's polite *when* and poured down the flood

as though it were hot tea over the back
of a hand, the weathervanes of the world
were repeatedly rusted still and torn free.

Look there, one still shakes a negative,
a panicked indecision, its shape one moment
a crowing rooster, or pointing dog,

or human palm, the next a pile of dust blowing
away beneath a lightning rod. The house,
strangely quiet, is suddenly unable to foretell

weather in anything but the most immediate fashion.

VIOLIN

Here is a mildly frightening thought:
most representations
of Hell have a sky. If only we could

alert whoever parents the gods
that their cruel children
have somehow obtained matches

and a magnifying glass. A bomb
in the stroller, mustard gas
and snakes in the can of soda,

a foreign-language luminary in the back
of the limousine:
these are the things it will kill us

to see. The statues that line the paths
of the campus where
children are trained to be prodigies

need a good massage, need to learn
how to loosen up.
Were every child given a violin

and set before the royalty of Europe,
would there still be
royalty? Which young one was it

who asked the professor: *If Heaven is*
the opposite of Hell,
does that mean they will forever be

dousing your intestines with water, applying
strips of skin to your tongue,
regurgitating your organs, doing work

for you? Only now are the strangers
getting the point of it:
it's dangerous to talk to children.

KITE

What are we teaching our children when
we caution against wax wings
yet give them kites that get tangled

in the overhead wires? A man's fingers shake,
belying the stillness he feels.
Is it some process, he wonders, some rushing

of blood to some unreachable destination,
functioning without his consent?
As much as he feels he's stopped, must he go on?

That sound of a kettle boiling is the sea,
that breaking of glass, the sky.
In the cries of newborns some of us

in tune with the future can already hear
whispers of death.
Who will keep us from our shame

by enfolding us within his own? Who will
name his skull Infamy, claiming
those who dwell within its ethereal walls?

Nobody said this was how it had to be,
but none spoke against it either.
What responsibility do we have to the road

ahead as opposed to that beneath our feet?
Who will act as scout,
that lonely occupation for which one

receives a parade at the outset
and is stoned on return?
How can we resist so rhythmic a tide

except by drowning? How can we resist
the wind if we rule out erosion?
The broken record still plays for half a revolution.

Nature, the philosopher says, *is engaged*
in a hunger strike on our behalf.
The stillness at the core of this moment

is identical to that which falls immediately
after an orator's last words:
the perfect instant when the last waves

of physical sound have flooded past
the last listener's ears;
the moment when those assembled have not

yet decided whether to burst into applause
or trample one another in panic,
each flapping limb tangling with the next,

the boughs of a tree being knotted by a hot wind.
Hell, he says, *is yet ravenous,*
and it won't be full until you get there.

ANCHOR

Here he comes, this man whose approach
could kick up a dust cloud in a land of fens, this man
who flings himself into the lives of others

as though a shell shot from beyond
the horizon, this man of few words, but all these.
Perhaps we should cut the world's flagpoles

in half and be done with it. The penitent have taken
to licking the floors and bedsheets
in leper colonies, to bathing last in the cold water

left after a long line of plague victims
have been washed for burial. The words *apathy*
and *sympathy* are claiming a relationship

to *pathology*. The planet is a pill in a pestle
and night is the shadow of the approaching
chemist. A ship of flour drops an anchor

of salt off a shore of sugar, the ocean
eroding all three quickly enough that before
the men can disembark they find themselves lost

at sea. Cream refuses to mix with coffee, apples
stay green and sour, leaves cling to the trees and die
without turning, fiddleheads fail to unfurl

into ferns and the loam of the forest floor is bathed
in sunlight. Pavement never cracks
and thousands of students go unemployed,

pens around the world simultaneously run dry
and ink pots tip, the sun stops directly overhead,
rendering sundials useless and stealing

from humanity the ability to check hairstyles
without the use of a mirror! Coincidentally, the foam
of ale that clings to the inside rim

of one young woman's pint glass relates,
in the original Arabic, the adventures
of Scheharezade's fifth cousin. In the distance,

a pulsar lets out one long burst that shows no sign
of subsiding; the planet's astrology community
is decimated. The elderly are disposed of

in landfills, tamped down into mineshafts
with heavy machinery. Legs and arms stick out
everywhere. Maybe the war crimes tribunals

of the future will charge invaders
with littering. The juries should be comprised
of children to ensure

swift and remorseless death
for the convicted. Buried beneath the forest floor,
a protesting monk rings a bell over and over

as he meditates towards his death,
a surprising two weeks later. *The gods,* he says,
are drinking a tea boiled over the embers

of our homes and bones. The people
bearing witness in the jungle above
likely don't notice the final chime of his bell,

their ears carrying on the task of listening
long after he has fallen over cross-legged onto
his side. Yes, here he comes, and when

he finally arrives, this man will preach the dangers
of loving in an end-time, when events decide
the length and quality of bliss and retaliation

becomes the institution which governs
all relationships. In return for his wisdom
let us feed and bathe him and clothe him

in the trappings of a king, let us prepare
a great gallows from which he can be hung,
let us wait patiently for a rent to form in the earth,

into which he shall be thrown, our own anchor of flesh.

CAGE

A period of least resistance is upon us. Quickly,
finish everything! Only nothing
may be left undone. Do you now find it

impossible to look strangers in the eye
without speculating where
the surgeon's pen might mark their forehead

with the crosshairs of future incisions?
In an infinite number of books
written by one monkey at one typewriter

where only one key still works, it states that
someday some intrepid explorer
will follow the overhead ducts to their source,

and the darkness that sweeps the edges
of our understanding
will be mapped. The wall around

this garden is a metaphysical one,
an insurmountable idea
that keeps us out and Heaven in. Assuming

our bodies will be left where they fall,
which do you bet
will eat us first, the birds or the worms?

Will the worms eat us and in turn
be eaten by birds? Will we climb
the food chain from the inside? Will we rise

as though a gorge, as though a hand reaching up
from the depths of the lion's throat?
Are these questions pointless, or are they

points without question? Hell-on-earth
has been in the planning since
shortly after heaven-on-earth was abandoned.

Maybe all this worry can be cured,
perhaps we are suffering
without need, maybe the answers we wish

would find us already have, are resting
on the backs of our tongues,
waiting for a cool drink of water. There is

a difference between a prison and a cage,
though such subtleties are lost
on some. We are now tied together, friend,
in modes more unfortunate than blood.

PIKE

Enjoy these light-headed moments
because eventually your
eyes will feel as heavy as stones.

Each half-year is only a nickel
of the decade:
would that we were richer still, or more miserly.

We are sailing these unknown seas
in a medicine bottle;
we are steering with a slender pestle.

Look out there on the street: our children
run amok, playing ball
with the helmets of our soldiers,

pouring water and goldfish
into the airtight bowls
favoured by our astronauts.

The city's buildings are thick incense sticks
against the cobalt sky
and the wind is blowing the scent

of their burning across the countryside.
The only way to digest this
is to mimic the birds and swallow

enough broken stones to help.
Is the pike all this news
comes down a pointed pole

on which rests the head of a rebel leader,
or just another kind of fish?
Begin, O cosmic weavers, to spin your loom

and make for us toques and flannel.
The weathermen say
it's going to be a hell of a winter

and there are still so many repairs
to reckon with.
The bellies of our men are barely covered.

Try to look on the mystery of life
as a playing card might:
it is natural to be shuffled and dealt.

We may still be resting and playing today
but tomorrow is Monday,
and on Monday everyone has to work.

Only at the maddest party is the talk
of retribution
and only at a funeral does no one speak.

If the old texts are right and nothing
but a column
of smoke holds up the heavens,

then we must all work together
to keep the fires burning
so Paradise might never fall to Earth

and we might never be crushed
under bliss.

STATUE

Suddenly the statuary is upon us,
hovering with panicked airs.
Why didn't we notice it sneaking up?

Guilt has unexpectedly become tangible,
is falling from its bearers
in tears of marble and limestone;

shall we rebuild the cracked white pillars,
the chipped plinths?
Shall we quarry here in the light

and air above ground? Free
of the weight of fault,
might we finally shoot into the sky

as we were obviously destined to?
Or, without ballast,
will we tip at the crest of the next wave?

What is the danger of speaking
against this in one's head?
That someone might be listening?

It was a good but rocky world
as recently as yesterday.
It is there to see in all the papers of record,

in all the shadows painted on the walls
of our caves. What was bound
to happen? This. Despite how unlikely

the events of our fall may seem,
there was always
a hundred percent chance

things would turn out this way. Prophecy,
it seems, is almost always just
an unrestrained case of history envy.

(Painfully the mountains sing of emptiness;
grudgingly the oceans
                                        do not.)

BEAR

Shall we treat the serpents to blood from our necks?
Shall we open our skulls so the monkeys might feast?

Shall we pick the fruit of our eyes and feed them

to one another as though they were cored sour apples?
These models we've made of the universe

turn it to stone, create the equivalent of a stuffed bear

rising in the corner of a gentleman hunter's study,
ferocious and snarling for all time, yet utterly powerless

to frighten those who believe it to be dead.

FLAG

It makes more sense now to use
the white flag we've been saving as a tourniquet,
and when we peel it

from the empty arteries of the dead
its mottled stains will sign a next, lonely nation.
Sing to the new children:

O children leaping from our heads,
O birth without pain, O minds emptied quick
as tipped urns!

Might we touch one another and be
revealed? In the murky dark between rooms
the business of inheritance continues.

Hold your tongue, my hands seem to be full.

MINEFIELD

Brush holly on this mess, brush oak,
treat the land with a poultice
of holy water and wort,

heal the holes in the ground with salves
made of moss and earth.
Use fireweed, use morphine, use hemlock,

stuff the craters with dark soil
and the seeds of wildflowers.
Replace Your Divots! the sign reads

at the mouth of the minefield.
One day we will decorate
with beehives and razor blades.

One day we will coat the walls
with various combinations of excreta.
One day water will refuse to blast

from the mouths of canons
and protestors will run wild,
and the buildings so calculatingly cleaned

of nuclear shadows will accumulate
the Bacchanal silhouettes of a riot.
The helmet on this head is a pea,

has stopped a bullet,
but the head rests on a spike
instead of a neck.

Dear Lord, they removed the chain
from his tongue and replaced it
with a ball of surgical steel.

He now speaks twice as often,
but only half as well. Each gulf, each pit,
each cavity and its accompanying stain,

each ghostly limb of a passer-by,
those partial absences, beg us to question
whether there will ever be another Rome,

another Sumer, Xanadu, Bethlehem.
Whether there has ever been
a presence with our best interests in mind.

BOOK

A tattered storybook found in the dirt
relates the tale of an awful ogre

who ate his employer because the six-figure
salary he received was one girl short

of what he requested. *There once was*
a six-armed goddess, another begins,

who still felt she needed an extra hand
around the house . . .

In the middle of the last story, a man
we all know is described in embarrassing detail:

he worked all his life to get himself
a trophy wife only to realize years later

she was for third place. Also in the dust
is a survival manual that when opened

only repeats the word *Run!* over and over
and over. Beside each book is another,

and another: a graveyard of philosophy,
mathematics, fairy tale, physics,

ethics, science fiction, sociology, language.
Do you think Fate, one heavier tome asks,

stepped back from her work one day
and was surprised to find a pair of blue jeans

on the loom? From this distance
it's hard to tell whether she was the kind

of craftsman whose concentration rests
at the needle or on the swatch of fabric

stretching into the distance.
If you want to broaden your horizons,

says the volume on Zen, *go live on a hill.*
Sleep is a form of time travel. The soul

works like a yo-yo. Heaven and Hell
both last only an instant, but death is the end

of our ability to perceive time.
Everyone remain calm!

                    There is one useful bit
not found in any text on the ground:

the sails of those six ships on the horizon
have had the centres cut from them.

Even with a good wind,
they can't land anywhere near here soon.

There is no need for all this panic, all this hope.

REEF

Cooling, the Earth is still cooling.
Feel it in the soles of your feet?
Press your cheek against the soil.

That sound you hear is the creak
and groan of flame
becoming stone. The children

have escaped and are rampaging across
the land. There is nothing
to do but wait to see which dies first:

their anger, their interest, or them.
Relax, we are indeed
still in the seventh day. When the mail

drops through the slot, everyone stops
talking and turns,
giving the conversation over

to silence, as one does on entering
a library, a bunker,
a tomb. Let us build

only with porcelain and spider web,
let's hang the rice paper moon
from a lute string, mount the yolk of sun

on a glass pedestal, perforate the night
with the hatpins of glorious ladies
and look down on our delicate world.

The uneasiness is settling,
an entropy of mood;
things are looking up, and not in fear.

The paper airplanes are flying again,
the zeppelins are brightly coloured
and say *Happy New Year* on the side,

the automobiles crashing into one another
on the street only bounce
away and run off cometing sparks.

Somewhere a train runs
on time. That tanker
that ran aground on the coral reef

was empty; there are children swimming
with penguins in the shelter
its bulk provides from the tireless surf.

Do yourself a quick favour:
look around. All the exits
are choked with the bodies of those

who realized it was time to flee
before you. There's nothing
wrong with spinning out of control

when, for once, you've been given
                                        enough space.

CRANE

By which road did they come,
the one through the jungle
or the one through the desert?

The one through the mountain pass.
Ah, it is open again?
It is open to them. All roads are open

to them? They don't require roads.
They seldom use them?
They float above all roads, they move

as the crane flies; all roads lead
somewhere and, with a little
thought, here could be somewhere.

By which road did they leave,
the one through the mountain pass
or the coastal highway? Again,

even in leaving, they use no roads.
Their steeds don't touch the ground?
They own no horses, sit no saddle.

Then why must our ears be covered
at the thunder of their approach?
They are as silent as the stars. Then why

do our ears ring with the detonation
of their departure? It is your lot.
What then is this confusion we see

playing itself out on the horizon?
What you see roiling there is
smoke, not clouds; sunset, not flame.

from

The Rush to Here

Nightwood Editions
2007

Sit still and enjoy the art. Your turn is today.

THIS IS NOT YOUR STORY

The soft applause of snow on the window
has left you with the impression of being
watched, and staring through the proscenium
of the brow bone, it's obvious the actor

and audience both consider the foreground
to be ahead of them. Looking forward
two seasons, longing for warmth, reading ahead;
did you come this far by action or momentum?

There's a haze around the thaw, a general sense
of doubt abroad. The world turns back to the sun
and shows the play of your well-wintered mind
to be closed to the idea of new light.

You turn the pages but find no end to the script.
This is how you know it's not your story.

REARVIEW MIRROR

The wind comes in and startles hair and scarves,
blowing them shitcrazy before letting them lead
with the controlled attention of snapping flags.

From a distance it looks like you're headed
into each other, but as you grow closer,
you see the original navigation

was off, that what appeared to be a line
is revealed as a plane, and closing in
requires more than momentum in one direction.

I flee constant change now, but know there are bound
to be days so steady I'll shake out a rearview
mirror's backward glance, just to remember desire.

You get a clear day out here and it truly shows.
You can't see forever, but as far as is fair.

A MOMENT'S AUTOGRAPH

Still enough sky-glow left to distinguish
colour, even as the trees descend
through the registers of green and the stoop
becomes shrouded and difficult to discern.

From a crack in the dark wall hang loose wires:
give a tug and watch society start
to unravel. There's no real need to begin
worry, just be aware where the pulling leads.

We use the same yellow diamond to sign
Elderly cross here as we do *Falling rocks*;
the colossal meteor that astounds
observers burns a moment's autograph.

Apprehension may settle around us like dusk
but the telescopes still capture first light.

DAYS OF GLASS

These are the days of glass, each pane clear
enough to show what's beyond, yet stacked up
against one another, they begin to blur.
Faint warps, lone motes of dust, fingerprints raised

in ghostly stains; each insignificant
and nearly clear to the unaided eye,
but seen through, back to back, and in quantity,
twisting distance into a barrier to sense.

Lined up like atoms in a brick, these unseen
flaws wait, and the further you try to look
through, the better odds what's next will be missed.
Polish them as you like, see what you see.

This dust can only be cleaned by hammer.
To reach the quick, one must go through the nail.

DRAWING IN WATER

Sometimes it feels like drawing in water,
painting the air with a bare light bulb.
You emerge from wet sleep, a submarine
breaching the ocean's skin in a flower

of froth, a vertical blast before falling
spent to float on the surface. That first breath,
vital to divers and whales both, drawn up
with all the panicked drama of drowning,

is a gasp of memory as much as need.
Labour at sifting this muddled mind's tea
for leaves telling a future's penury.
It's like drawing in water, this steeping.

The scalding dark a cetaceous waiting
for light, and the surfacing breath to come.

DITCH

How many feet was it in front of my home
that I fell in the ditch that opening night
fifteen years back, drunk and rank of some town
girl's perfume? The bank and weeds' tall theatre

drew a blackout curtain over my prone
form and swayed, a shushed and respectful crowd
viewing a well-known/well-appointed corpse
laid out in the roadside's funeral home.

From a civil bed to the misty primal;
spin me, stars, until I am erect.
Take me by the neck like a mother would, that first
clutch at the nape, lift me to your breast.

Dumb, the cars' searchlights passed my dim cradle.
Dumber still, I lay agape and slept.

AUTOMATIC DOORS

It's true: I'm too fast for automatic doors.
The buildings above are incidental ladders
to unoccupied spaces, cubic gates,
blue framed off from blue. Your mouth a chute

out which language spills past ellipses of teeth
(not a bridge between thoughts, but a trailing off . . .)
I try to stay open to these insults,
glass doors that will break before pulling aside.

Your throat seals with indignity, closes
like a piece of lost applause, your tongue
swells with biting, your mandible locks
and your teeth grind only absent words.

Seeking a higher power means, sincerely,
I climbed these stairs just hoping for more than yours.

THE UNEQUAL GAZE

The unequal gaze like an empty page keeps
me motionless, but also keeps me honest,
anxious, docile. Nice and fortified.

Through evolution we've become so upright
that we're nearly falling over backwards.
This old stereoscopic erection

fine when rearing up to scan the plains each way
for predators, but not so pleasant
when the predators use it in reverse.

M. Foucault, I think I know what you mean
when you say *visibility is a trap.*

You'd think I'd be ready to ambush
the power, but I still worry I'm being watched.

THE DEVIL

Run, Fucker. Run like the Devil is horny
and you're the last man standing on Judgment Day.
There's nothing on your tail now but age and night
and still the highway stretches on so hard.

Eat, run, don't you dare look at those exits,
their gaping mouths. He's coming, building,
working the edges of your establishment.
Who ever gave you permission to exist?

Fatigue is just a step towards thrill,
and standing means you're alive, at least for now.
No one can tell you how things will be later,
but being the last piece of meat, you please

his sense of timing now. The pendulum starts rocking,
and the Devil, boy, he lives for the sound of ticking.

TRUCK STOP GOTHIC

Once I cooked in a greasy roadside spoon,
just like this, and during one rotten
lunch rush swiped my stainless steel knife
at a passing fly, cutting its head clean off,

right through where a neck should be. I felt divided
at realizing this truck stop gothic dream,
and without thinking went back to slicing
toasted western triangles in a trance.

Where were you that day? What did you have for lunch?
I apologize if it was you who got
that order: such an incisive dish,
well-dressed with a pickle. You understand.

And the quick death hiding in the bread's darkness?
Sorry you tasted such greatness and never knew.

MANY WORLDS

Sure, there may be other universes,
as many as there are options at all

given moments, branches from branches
until choice becomes more bush than tree,

but in some ensuing universes
most everything stays the same as in this one:

a butterfly tilts to another bearing,
the old lady turns left instead of right,

you spend an extra night alone with the lust
that keeps you lonely, and nothing new comes

of it, no catastrophic difference
felt, no recognizable consequence made.

There are many worlds we can't tell from our own
because some choices don't matter at all.

A SILENT FILM

If he comes to the rail like a child called
to mother, like a trireme's marine spying
land after the panic of losing sight
of the coastline, if he comes when beckoned,

is he still to be punished? Someone shows
a silent film against a billowed sail,
the storm gives up rain and lightning in sheets.
On orders the oarsmen watch and refuse to act.

The children make chalk outlines of themselves
on the pavement, what would be called angels
in other weather. Parents and guardians
look on, filled with the love and selflessness

expected by their televisions.
From the sea, a call for help comes by radio.

A SET OF DEADLY NEGOTIATIONS

Lately, all your walks begin as though pushing
back the table from a set of deadly
negotiations. Luck doesn't hold
or run out, it's farmed and subject to a life

governed by its own rain and sun, factors
finite maths can't calculate: the stock boy
lecturing the farmer on the minutiae
of sowing. Little bites of Everyman,

tiny cannibalisms of everyday:
lips chewed in indecision, nails bitten
with angst, a sucked thumb's banality,
the knocked nose's long, coppery drink.

Don't let a morning's blank reverie
become a pleasant evening's lack of sleep.

RUSH

Spectacles, testicles, wallet and watch;
if only the body could catch up with the blood.
I'm always chasing this heart's last rapid tick,

drawing near an invisible finish line
over which I can step and stop the clocks,
have a drink and settle down to make some kin.

Nice town and I've never seen it, nice faces
but I can't think of how the names relate.
We win this race of confrontations,

invent promising strategies, learn to tell
better stories: wings lift shoes, a boat rows
in the clouds, the quarrel meets the apple.

Know what I forgot in the rush to here? Blood
isn't just inside me, it is me, my brother.

WAR MEMORIAL

Some old men in their front gardens make me
want to nod assurance, say, *Yes, I see you*

in there; say, *This fumbling is just another*
set of lanky teen years, a weedy version

of you tripping over your changing feet,
all elbows and disproportioned legs,

prickly posture and misfitting clothes, living
through another awkwardness of being.

On the war memorial the kids
climb, skate, and sit, eroding the old

plinth down to marble bones and epitaph;
their claims on *now* staked with ass and graffiti.

Near the street, a soldier in uniform sells poppies,
having long ago made his peace with the thistles.

SILENCE IS A DEAD LANGUAGE

Silence is a dead language. Forward
letters you don't want to deal with on to friends
you know need the attention. Be bold:
the sun's at your back down those dim alleys.

When you throw pieces of yourself into
the world, do you consider it discarding
or decorating? No gesture outside
religion seems uncluttered enough.

What you're looking for is ingenuity
enough to let ambition go: to find
yourself building the simple, the clever,
suddenly satisfied with what's appearing

at the ends of your much-surprised hands.
Listen: the silence ends. Raucous applause.

ALL THE STANDARD CANDLES

Lately, you're at a loss to articulate.
There are no chances to think of what to say,
only opportunities to speak,
the mouth a channel for impatience,

the mind a parking lot for desire.
As though a drop of mercury introduced
to the ear, your memories unmoor, want
to slip past one another like strangers.

Weigh this day against all the standard candles,
each moment's magnitude and distant
memory. Is it a failure to see all stars
as points of blurred light: remote, vague, aloof?

Your mind tells you whom you should recognize,
but your eye's not naked enough to place them.

EXIT STRATEGY

Tell me there is a way to believe it all,
an exit strategy with groggy murmurs
of nothing but rest and a quiet universe.

All I can think of is my child, asleep
in bed, dealing with whatever birthright
his dreams afford his fears, waiting to wake.

Sometimes I feel like Kepler, poised to inherit
pages of wrinkled data, but grumbling,
What a holy-fucking mess Tycho left behind.

Under the surface of the crowd's rumble
is a song. We could have danced, you know,
to the how-not-why of these perfect heartbeats.

It's true. You've not been asked to understand.
You've been asked to listen, and work it out.

MOSTLY THE WORLD WAITS

The vandals here paint with fire, masters
every one. If only that which stands
before us is true, no wonder old men
marshal armies. Mostly the world waits

patiently. Mostly people get on
with things. Mostly they are unaware
of waiting. Mostly they find themselves in
an attractive space of unconscious

hope. Mostly the end arrives and leaves
without notice. The sky is not falling.
It is a suspended canopy,
hung from high-tensile airplane cable rising

into spaces we can only see at night.
Sit still and enjoy the art. Your turn is today.

GO

I sit in my day as though it is made
of bone china, eyes shifting from tock to tick
as if the weight of a rested glance might break
the view into pieces. Gone are all instants,

and in place, memory. The night was a bull
with six banderillas in its flank, a mad
wolverine caught in the corner and harassed,
a dog stumbling in the last moments of rabies.

To lie down and sleep under a full wolf moon
and end the quiet effort with snow;
I have seen the heart in your eyes shine
with the fever of loss and doubt, squalling.

You wondered how long this could continue.
You held on quite some time. I saw. Good night. Go.

from *Whiteout*

ECW
2012

Remember, this is only a test.

DANTE'S SHEPHERD

(Inferno, Canto XXIV, Lines 1–15 Revisited)

At dawn I walk to the bank in the rain,
hood-peak pinned with one blue hand and wrist
forced from its sleeve (while its twin does not deign

to ditch the cuff, but hides instead, a fist
worrying, a clenching/unclenching tide,
mulling its wish to progress and subsist).

The sky clears itself while I am inside,
scuttling the dull clouds of a coastal morning
for white litter on blue with sun cockeyed.

It leans down on the hills as though scorning
any doubt that the universe still lives
without my happiness in bloom, warning,

Look down at those matching hands: where one thrives,
flush with life, if stiff and warming, the other,
also red and aching, only now arrives.

THE NEW WEATHER

Just before the key catches in the lock
a snowflake lands on your eyelash and blurs
the scene; stretching the instant an instant
longer, slurring outer and inner worlds.

A moment, a moment more; you dare not move,
and so pause on the sill, wait for the tear
that will form in either the new weather
hot from the house, or your eye's open stare.

BRUSHFIRES

(February 2009)

There are always bodies to discover
at each new disaster, in a range of states,
from seeming sleep to a charred disorder.

But once the inspections begin in earnest,
expect this death count to escalate
as the scorched landscape is closely assessed,

teeth and DNA separated, filed
as discrete, razed histories, aggregates
of last moments and final acts, the wild

fires closing in, their inverse-shadows
cast by a speeding sackcloth sun; innate
desire to touch, like first love, pupils aglow.

It's common enough to come across pairs
of bodies, dumped freight washed up in the surf,
broken on the pavement beneath barely

there buildings, or even camouflaged
in the charcoal and atomized silicate
of a brushfire, but harder to tell which vague

strewn ember was once man or woman,
or which was both; entwined in conjugate
burning, the heat put to use and flames fanned.

Falling or burning, embraced against the end;
what-was-once-two closes in, supplicates,
smoulders down to one corpse, crumbles, ascends.

FUSE

Between every two people runs a fuse,
a line from head to heart or heart to crotch,
cunt to mouth, eye to navel, hand to throat;
short or long, strung this way or that,

welding one desire to another love, one
need to another want, hate to deeper hate,
fear to loyalty, tremble to light touch,
flame to a bucket, fall to a turned back.

What's unique isn't its length or course,
whether travelling from one side or both,
or even who's stood at either end,
but ignition: just how and when it got lit.

COWBOY STORY

The books sit on the shelf, a row of coma patients
in a ward, a series of selves no longer able to learn
and trapped at the point of injury: the last page.

At the donor clinic I offer my arm to the spigot
of the needle and think, as I see the bag fill with
blood, *there goes some of me*. But that's a lie:

as soon as it exits, the fluid is its own object,
with all the attendant foreignness and filthy infection
that implies and has no meaning in terms of me.

Life happens like a cowboy story in which two lines
of gun-wielding men walk slowly towards each
other, skinning those smokewagons until the sky is white

with exploded gun powder. Out in the open, shooting
past all logic, they advance until either reality is killed
or they fall. I'm not saying there's no control,

but rather that control is all there is. Keep reading
to find out how it ends. The only cover offered is
the bad aim of enemies, and an adherence to the script.

THE SNAILS

I.

And the rain keeps the sidewalk dark this morning,
an inverse Red Sea, water parting the desert
you walk to work—your mind engaged ticking
off obligations. And if you could picture

the last two hours of struggle as one minute,
a line of snails would burst from the green verge
like a salute of mistimed starters' bullets,
loping into leads and losses for the curb—

each corkscrew staircase shell a leaning sail
in a yacht race—the wind tilting this miniature
Exodus as it aims at an invisible
Promised Land. And some imperative Nature

has yet to explain to us draws them over
the concrete path we haven't yet explained to Her—
bodies scoured on the drying foundation,
eyestalks strained at some strange salvation.

2.

Sleep's void gives way to a quality of light
that yields to the dawn's sense of duty—
and night cedes to day without space to admit
what's been lost in both time and beauty.

Fingers count in pockets—two-thirds of life
pledged to sleep and slow minds—and I predict
what promise remains will fail, humbled by lies
and cheques, both of which have become my product.

I fear I was mistaken, that I misspoke,
misheard, was unaware of the complex nature
of the situation—I leapt and broke, before I
looked, just what did not need fixed.

Habit and a path lead my morning walk,
and each hour that I tap on the stone of this clock
keeps water flowing and the Egyptians at bay,
but still leads to Jordan's bank as ordained.

3.

And amidst this well-composed painting of speed
sit odd wrecks, fragmented spirals cutting
through wet bodies—smashed chariots in a sea
of reeds—broken, not drowned. And it's not cunning

or God that saved some over others, but chance—
the feet of those keen or restless few
on their way to work ahead of you advanced
despite the slow story playing below.

And whether they did or didn't care,
and whether following under orders
or fleeing under orders, and whether
some even enjoyed the slight pop of life under

foot, you can't know. You're moving through the race
as one does a book, at a historian's pace—
wondering how, between catastrophic fate
and divine interest, life ever lasts the day.

SONG FOR MEMORY

The old men are proud of their jukebox picks,
Humming in time where the words come unfixed,
Just five kings left, only four can turn tricks,
The tallow burns down to a bath for the wicks.

Some get it right while some make mistakes,
Some hear the chorus, some just the break,
Some mouth the verse through sips that they take,
Some rub their chins like their memories ache.

The harbour's socked in, the lighthouse is on,
And row upon row of the people they know
Stand still as a choir with the audience gone.

A full house is five men, but very few glances,
They shuffle the cards and hand out the chances,
Eye all the queens while the clock still advances,
And ponder their time in long empty trances.

Stuck in the space where their reach meets the view,
Where last thoughts hold on, but the first are too few,
They crackle like fire on its way up the flue,
Give what's deserving its day and its due.

The hands keep turning to follow the dawn,
And row upon row of the people they know
Stand still as a choir with the audience gone.

The fog has blown off, but still hangs in the lung,
A guitar's in the corner, its neck left unstrung,
The girl at the bar is impossibly young,
But the brass gets its wipe, and the pints still get slung.

No head goes unnodded, no head goes unhung,
The time to go home has long ago come,
The song goes around on its black vinyl tongue,
And row upon row of the people they know
Stand still as a choir that hasn't yet sung.
Stand still as a choir that hasn't yet sung.

PAREIDOLIA

The couple in the basement argue in the space
they've rented and we can hear every word:
shouted, spoken, or hissed through bitten lips.

From the patterns of paisleys on the wallpaper
faces emerge, grotesque little Mandelbrots
that once viewed cannot be unseen.

Constellations break into asterisms and form
bodies, flatbreads show saviours,
windows reflect a variety of virgins.

We sit quietly, hoping and dreading the fight
will finish before they reach and resolve
some issue of our own, saving us the trouble.

Makes me wonder what the people upstairs
think of these silent evenings at our desks,
and if those below hear aught from those below them.

EMERGENCY BROADCAST SYSTEM

This is only a test. At the long tone
we will begin. At the long tone we will end.
At the long tone it is time for the news.
At the long tone you may begin to write.
When the bell rings you may rise to leave.
When the bells ring you may choose to flee.
The strike of the clock marks another birth.
The strike of the clock leaves welts shaped
like hands. Striking the clock marks
another morning. As the short tone sounds
events will unfold. As the short tone sounds
the time will be right. At the bell you will begin
to salivate. The experiment will begin
when the toll reaches all ears. The experiment
will begin when the topless lady wrings
out the last of her clothes. The experiment
involves pealing and will be double blind.
There are two strips of cloth for each ding
you hear. Please put them on, then record
and report. Ignore the mewl of the cat
in the box. The mewl of the cat in the box
has no relevance. Whether alive or dead
at the end of the experiment, you must ignore
all complaints from the cat. Your first
responsibility is to the sound of the tone.
Forget the cat. Focus instead on the topless
lady. You have been provided with paper
for notes. You must take only the notes
that are sung to you. If you cannot hear
the notes, you may be shocked
by the provided visuals. The visuals
will provide some context, but will be shocking
for some audiences. The boom of the howitzer

may make you jump. The boom
of the howitzer will connote importance.
The silver trumpets' peal will announce
a king arriving or leaving. The chime
will call you in for tea and cake. The chime
is pleasant, but cannot be ignored.
As the chime sounds, birds will fall dead
from the trees. The chime will signal
your imminent passing from one bicycle
lane to the next. The klaxon will sound
loudly in warning. The klaxon also cannot be
ignored. The klaxon will note the start
of the baggage carousel. The horn will give
you the fright of your life. The ringing of metal
means swords have been drawn. The ringing
of metal can never be good. The trolley's clang
might remind you of something fond and sweet.
The trolley's clang might remind you
of your forgotten suitcase. The whistle of the train
means all are aboard and accounted for.
The whistle of the train used to be in the distance.
The whistle of the train now comes with a bright
light. At the long tone, the experiment is set
to begin. At the long tone you may begin to run.
Each pulse of your blood will count for one beat.
Each beat of your blood will be considered a long tone.
For today's purposes, each pulse of your blood
will be a starter pistol in the distance, through water,
and echoed. Remember, this is only a test.

OWED

My debts are my blessings, so I stay home
to count what I haven't and add no more.

The pots above the stove hang and ring
their slight touches as I enter the room.

Here are the facts of you alone, they sing.

The kitchen table is an accountant's desk.
Sit down without a plate, it says, among

the strewn toys and echoed noise of small wrecks.

Calculate not what's owed and owned,
but what's outstanding, and who that's for.

BLAZON FOR THE CRONE

For a skeleton there is a spinning wheel over which she is pulled;
for a heart there is a bucket, a well, a rope—

Her mind, a covered bridge, lets each memory rattle
its loose planks, grow in the corners like spiderwebs—

She is older than either paint or harebell, lime-ancient:
tuskless, yet still able to paw sand in anticipation—

Invisible inside, there is a curved retina, a fingertip's blunt
nerve ending, an eardrum pulled tight as embroidery—

Outside, her world is a tongue with tastebuds numerous
as strawberry seeds through which she moves, a glacier of salt.

SONG FOR A DIVORCE BUDGET

Two halfs don't always make a whole,
One can't always be split.
Three's not really good company,
Two can't tango worth shit.

Four is just not that fantastic,
Three can't pin down its roots.
Five's no longer so furious,
Four looks awful in suits.

Six is no beast when all alone,
Five does not a party make.
Seven ain't so lucky in love,
Six has no dice to shake.

Eight will never know it's enough,
Seven can't wait all week.
Nine won't dress to below the hilt,
Eight's not completely unique.

Ten can't live without decadence,
Nine won't be gauged in lives.
One ignores all lonesome numbers,
Zero loathes those who divide.

THE DEFINITION OF ZERO

The origin of any measurement; value
linking positive and negative;
completely obscured; the lowest point;
gone, not done; that which no longer lives.

Cross section of an empty egg; gun sight;
cardinal; gravity; digit; freezing;
clear; even, oddly; wholly precise in time;
absence of magnitude, and of phoneme.

Kamikaze engine between wings;
to aim; kill off; reduce to nil; alone;
none; naught; cipher; the thing in nothing;
that guy on the couch in the empty home.

TRAINING DAY

(September 2003)

In one hand, the paper with a photo of training
marines belly-down on the deck of a ship,
pointing black guns

out at an empty sea; in the other a mug of coffee
that's getting me through a half-read,
half-watched morning,

the first day of school laughing nervously across
the street. What are they aiming at out there
where nothing remains

still? From my sunroom it's impossible
to tell who will be what when
the evening breaks.

It would be nice to have such clear starts
again. Shooting the blue just to learn
how the gun stirs in your hands.

ICARUS IN THE WAX MUSEUM

Imagine the boy inversed, real feathers
        grafted to a wax body and winched
                up near the museum's halogen ceiling;

cutting through climate-controlled weather,
        starting to droop in the light, wrists pinched
                with cable, wingtips eye-screwed and wheeling.

When he liquefies, dripping on those below, his wings
        don't fly off, ascend on their own
                to some girdered bliss, but instead remain

caught in The Fall; the body's soft tallow
        drawn down, while its means of flight still drones
                on through an honestly human rain.

                (hubris isn't just about going up,
        but what falls back down)

He can't reach Heaven but neither will he find Hell,
        because we didn't just make his wings,
                but the sun, the sky, and the man as well.

ROSE

Surgery and injury kin, prune and plumb,
thorny trimmings piling up in the pot's saucer,
limbs stacked level to the grave's lip.

Cut and cut again, tree to bush to thumb
greened against those leaves unaware death's not
sensitive enough to know touch from grip.

Intake, sudden breath, beauty through pain's dumb
memory, the loss you know is a plot
compared to the wince you make with each snip.

STATE OF EMERGENCY

(September 2001 / January 2006)

I.

It's already snowed three feet when the newsman
approaches with his camera gear in tow,
looking for a degree of depth he can send
to the cables—the city's crumpled crow

knocked out on winter's frosted skyscraper,
men digging out cars, neighbours pitching in.
Strange comedy, this—part romance, part caper
—tragic and remote at times, but rich in

clownish annoyance. From the edge of my eye
he slides into view and holds out his mic
without the slightest word of civil invite—
a move that's my cue to stand and sigh, spike

the spade like Prospero's staff in the ashen
ice of the plough's latest pass at set design,
lean in wearily, smile in that sly fashion,
say—*It just keeps falling, but I'm doing fine.*

2.

Once I fled a burning shadow as it fell,
a poorly secured backdrop—aware each blink
could be the one that would extend, kill
the stage lights, let the darkness stretch out and drink

whatever strange draught my time was made of.
When the script said to run, I ran—helped those I could,
carried an old man up above
the dusty asphalt for a stretch—the twin snows

of shoes and foolscap-confetti falling
through a fog of crushed concrete, asbestos,
and disbelief. I sat for months mulling
that day's bizarre performance as best as

I could—a silent and foreign Caliban,
jaw-clenched and stunned, unwilling to cajole
from my twisted brain some actor's acumen,
while others got applause for a smooth *Let's roll.*

3.

I can't tell from this frozen window whether snow
or ash, nature or nurture, will bury
us at the roadside—but any rough weather's now
a good enough excuse for worry.

When the wind changes, who's obliged to speak?
When the sky is falling, who must be informed?
It makes bad theatre, this love of *heartbreak*
—fact overacted but underperformed.

Recite in the mic, a string of idle
words, three glass-eyed seconds of civic duty—
charmed, like Ariel's promise to make a bride
of Wonder for the arm of Chance and be set free.

A bird flies into the camera lens,
the storm hammers down, buildings fall—life leaves us
each speechless for once—well rehearsed, cleansed,
island-bound on stage, not reciting, but live.

WHITEOUT

Pull the car over and take a moment
to note that this is where the road ends,
notwithstanding the memory of the path
continuing around the bend. The last
red taillights are painted over and the snow
presses its face up against the window,
begging to be let in. Turn the engine off,
it says, and hear this original soft
sound, a book of white nothing. I am life
without known rules: no signs, no lights, no lines
on the road; no ditches, asphalt, or curbs;
no people to see, no horizons or turns
to make; no destination. Draw aside.
Let your engine die and we'll compromise
temperature, colour, sound. I am life
where life heaves, turns and reads its final leaf.
Inside, the tick-tock of cooling machinery;
outside, the rattle ends this needless scenery.
If the road goes on without you, it goes blind.
Here, all is only static and knuckles cracking;
here you ease the tension ahead by waiting,
despite the chance of being hit from behind.

CANTUS FIRMUS (SPRING MORNING)

Dear Lord, things are always already closing.
The sun is now over the hills and rising.
Daffs go ochre in the garden, crisping.
Age settles on the baby in teeth and talking.
The spider's presently pea-sized and growing.

A thought came to me through this accounting,
Subtle instance of near understanding.
A moment so sublime that in its writing
It disguised itself and hid in the waning
Beginning of this morning's latest ending.

from *Diversion*

ECW
2015

Is this thing even on?

#CIVILDISCONVENIENCE

What if Revelations had been called Revolutions?
Hang on a second while I google this.
Jesus laughed.
Fire breaks through the smoke the way sun breaks through the fog.
Quiet as an option silently dies.
Unforgettable facts wedge themselves like stains between our bedsheets.
Prayer's tinny voice squawks from an analog phone.
Most rioters eventually get distracted by mirrors.
I'd take *the calm before the storm* if it meant having any calm
whatsofuckingever.
There are levels of speechless we haven't yet discovered.
Wanking is the other white meat of art.
The forecast follows the fearcast.
Horror becomes the state one occupies when seeing oneself quoted in the news.
Marginalia declared autonomy and formed a state.
People in the suburbs suffer from Stock Home Syndrome.
Who dares enjoy themselves anymore?
Remember to thank Christ you don't have to get off your couch.
Saying things gets only saying done.
Flames paint outer walls red the way televisions paint inner walls blue.
Down-the-way is where news happens.
Pluck the bricks flying by to rebuild your house.
Listen for the constant exposition of a man sure he's nailing a date.
We have the right to demand boredom.
Lassie keeps barking about how much Timmy likes it down the well.
Sadness retains its title as anger's most widespread illusion.
It's become apparent your fantasies just aren't interesting enough.
Civil unrest always evolves into parties.
Police hunch over coffee with their heads bowed and gun hands twitching.
Rows of driveways straight as bars on windows.
A Streetcar Named Covet.
I just realized my dick and head both loll the same way when tired.
Dollarama looted but the bookstore left untouched.

Staff the barricades!
We used to say *don't go into the woods* whereas now we say *don't read the comments.*
Cave wall shadows only work if there's a fire.
It appears that *decimate* now means to reduce by a factor of *holy fuck*.
Can anyone tell whether it's kindness or malice that's reached homeopathic levels?
Allow me to apologize in advance for my humanity.
Type that line as though something depended on it.
Your door rattles in the jamb but the lock is sturdy and continues to hold.
The armchair uprising has begun.

#CLOCKWORKORRAGE

Come all you haters and see what I have wrought.
Our primary role as teachers is to demonstrate how to best waste time.
I survived Seamus Heaney and all I got was this lousy career.
Monuments are built daily to distraction.
The terms *rescuers* and *salvagers* are mostly interchangeable.
Before the sun has risen it is just a bright hill.
Only twenty-four men have walked on the moon and/or behind Jesus.
Crack the spine of the *Gutenberg Bubble*.
Statistically speaking there has to be a secret door around here somewhere.
Moses flicked his cigarette into the dead bush.
Plan your strategic withdrawal from wishing everyone a happy fucking birthday.
You have seventy-three important updates waiting.
A more likely zombie apocalypse would be a horde of abandoned buildings.
What we call the sociopaths among us is *neighbours*.
The number of Aboriginal women missing from this line is difficult to estimate.
Heaven don't want him and Hell's afraid he'll go Columbine.
Poets are the unacknowledged escalators of the world.
We all see dead people now.
The subtitles have been subtly lying to us for years.
Sleeper cells awaken and begin plotting in your spreadsheets.
Ennui is an alert that pops up to tell you there are currently no alerts.
The Illuminati left their lights on again.
Bombs strapped to our babies in their dear little TNT onesies.
A Room of One's Pwn.
If I had it to do all over again it would be a cookbook.
Simply breathing is moving forward.
Every breast exposed in the Sistine Chapel is a new big bang.
xx is right next to cc.
The emperor of YKK pulls himself together.
Look into the dead shark eyes of our leader. You are what you contract.
Violence has an exchange rate against the price of oil.
I heard about him but I never dreamed he'd have blue eyes and blue jeans.
Truly elegant equations deserve cartouches.

Naked old men in flip-flops roam the change room with their hanging
tits and balls.
Religion is like sucking in your gut while standing on the scale.
Glitter arcs from the TV remote.
There's been a sudden spike in the number of lives ended on knees in
front of a SWAT unit.
I want to die with my boots on or at least my slippers.
Hitler's ghost slow claps in the silence men call Hell.

#MARGINALPERSONALITYORDER

Starlings vomit song and call it nature.
Hollywood is rebooting its World History franchise to interest new audiences.
Lanced thought bubbles suppurate white space.
Starving children would eat Ebola if it came in noodle form.
Pockets as choked with clacking billiard balls as a porn star's mouth.
The traffic lights glow like new scabs.
Starlets keep longer in the oven than the freezer.
That's as fucked up and perfect as Freddie Mercury's overbite.
Magnetic poles speak magnetic Polish.
Hug that galaxy with open arms.
Chubby legs on a baby are the world's last honest pleasure.
That man with the plastic glasses never stops humming "Sonny's Dream."
Death is forever in the process of dying but never dies.
Politicians endorse the stupid fucking children.
Drunks stagger by in perfect stockings.
Always meet your mother in a public place far from home.
Clouds press down like a hand over your mouth.
Police are parked outside the neighbour's house but not doing anything.
Every stone is a fossil of something.
Those who don't listen closely are best shunned like a colony of leopards.
Blue chalk dust hangs like a breath before something long unsaid
Hurricanes swirl in the satellite photo like nature's bleached assholes.
It's hard to choose between the best popes.
Hungry people are more dangerous than starving people.
Spread flesh on the sheets like almond butter on bread.
Hunting for porn is now a kind of porn.
The next trick is getting all this AstroTurf to photosynthesize.
Accidental nakedness found in a gust of wind.
Time is a trellis on space's wall.
Professors keep fucking their students and teaching them lessons.
Narcissism is the DSM's Occam's razor.

Every word out of a royal's mouth shoots like spermless semen on the
world's face.
Boys fear women who refuse to fear men.
Practise first guessing first and second second.
The baby is almost as big as his Rambo knife now.
Sharpie on the stall door has lost its prophetic cred.
Don't pot the black ball just yet.
Announcements over the prison PA ping off suburban homes.
Neither smoking nor assfucking-without-a-preparatory-enema are
acceptable anymore.
Rifle envy is slightly less creepy than handgun envy.
Diagnose *this* motherfucker.

#OUTLIARS

It is time to shit in the houses of our dearest friends.
Listening to a child coughing in bed is virtually anxiety-free for me.
Pigeons anoint our monuments with reality.
To-do lists fall over you like shovelfuls of grave dirt.
Given it was a telephone wire you sat on I can't figure out how it is
    your pants caught fire.
Our ears crackle as societal pressure changes.
Research all the surprising places the clitoris ends up going.
Origami cranes flock to the watering hole to find only ink.
The solar system is a Venn diagram of decreasingly unrelated ideas.
I bought my soul back from the pawn shop for twice what it's worth.
Heaven and Hell stake out opposite ends of the living room and stare
    each other down.
Imagine the throbbing anger that is the Hulk's cock.
Rogue currencies exchange significant glances.
Oulipo is poetry's BDSM.
My cappuccino foam looks like an ass crack I'd like to fuck.
The farmer comes in from the field and wipes the bitcoin from his hands.
Bracketed counters beside folder icons tick up faster.
Look at all the loose feet in this massacre photo.
I insist that this in fact *is* formal.
BabyGap is clothes made by babies for richer babies.
Tremolo wisdom warbles from a dozing pothead.
Volume control is a future civil rights issue.
Stick your finger up Saturn's rings and let's call ourselves hitched.
Taxis pull up to the crashed planes to wait for fares.
Run away with me from the tumbling buildings.
Who else was stoned to death today?
I hope God is happy now.
Give blood every six weeks whether or not you can find a clinic.
Every idea taken from below like a seal by a killer whale or a reverse
    cowboy.
Austerity is what's *Owed on a Grecian Earn*.

Blinking first is what liars do last.
My sons will never know a world without a mute button.
Flinch at the thought of a ~~poetry reading~~ broken dick.
That rollercoaster-dip feeling of a plane in turbulence is now an every-
where feeling.
Death's no biggie.
2.718281828459045235360287471352662497757247093699959574966967
Floor to ceiling windows look out onto the tops of your cheeks.
Latest crack smoking video is actually of a fissure leading straight to Hell.
Truth's unit of measure is the telomere.
Forget poetry and just enjoy the unbridled collecting and hoarding of
every last thing.
There'll be time enough for the important stuff when I'm dead.

#UCAN'TDOUCHETHIS

Let's burn this fucking planet to the ground.
Mood is a disease.
There's a dumpster parked in the Anglican cemetery.
At the centre of the question lives the Minotaur with his axe and raised eyebrow.
Everyone's still looking at us white guys but it just doesn't feel the same.
Sharpen the planks of your placards into stakes.
Tiny distances don't just belong to Zeno.
Someone keeps asking us to show him our tits.
This is not what I intended.
Death's character was the first one added to the book.
The answer to *Which cosmological structure are you?* is *All of them.*
Einstein's Cross gets worn around every neck.
Parachutes covered in a series of interconnected zippers.
An Ali punch thrown underwater would still knock you the fuck out.
Being is the wound and the body its scar.
Lineups at the McDonald's are ten times those at the church.
Texts chirp in an effort to fuck your eyes.
As usual men continue to explain their ownership of you.
There's always the option to just draw the underwear on with a Sharpie.
Polite conversation murmurs its Muzak.
The musk of men in a January elevator has no solution except the
building's destruction.
We are always walking the Planck.
The truth can only be explained in powers of ten.
Flowers on the bush of possibility are called news items.
Don't let your invented marginality become a fetish.
Rhythm originates in the sunglasses.
Immune systems line themselves up against all the wrong battlefronts.
The planned blood transfusion from a shark goes off without a hitch.
Vibrations rattle up the flagpole that is scale.
Retarded guys sometimes just want to chat.
The tiniest movements of the feet are now considered dance.
Vaccines could have outlived their purpose.

All your accusations fail because you don't know me.
I look into each of your eyes and am disgusted by the hatred and want
reflected there.
Excised human heart flesh soaked in warm seawater will try to beat.
Feminist tears taste just as salty.
Space smells like the barbeque at a NASCAR tailgate party.
A goth tanning salon opens at midnight.
There's nothing left to be done except concentrate on the children.
If we could tunnel through history the answer would reveal itself every
step of the way.
Alright stop with the Hammertime.

#THEKNOWNUNIVERSACE

Love flattens time.
The groceries in the trunk hyperventilate beneath the locks.
Old men substitute video games for bathing.
It's a vegetarian act to eat a carnivore.
The sum of the squares of the first seven primes is 666.
Practising disdain now constitutes sixty percent of billable hours.
Dice rattle in the breath as though the chest were a craps table and each lung a cup.
The convention centre is also a mortuary.
I owe my soul to the company whore.
A fat man jogs in time-lapse.
More effort goes into social media strategy than elevators.
Chinese knives lose their handles before the blades dull.
A thyroid lies naked in a dish.
The copyright text on sea salt flakes reads *Calvin Klein*.
Headaches keep a state of affairs more current than peace.
All the best meteors fall on Russia.
Heavy scent of makeup powder and cigarettes.
There are people who like to get liquored up before they go out to get liquored up.
Mirrors are a form of time travel.
An angel fakes a broken wing to draw predators away from its nest.
University degrees are chosen like earrings.
Your morals stepped out for a smoke and fell down drunk.
Red pants don't give a fuck.
Even the Vikings are zipping up.
It's lazy to seek converts when there are disciples to be had.
God is not yet Santa.
All the aprons and skillets and church bells are spattered with liquid rust.
Sometimes the only way to mask crossing yourself is in a nose wipe.
The Collected Dicks of Emily Poeminson.
Supermassive black holes draw in and push out like cunts in the night.
Gabriel's Horn is hatted by math.

There's no more room in the basket for heads.
Only at the end of the day does one notice one's glasses were filthy.
Cosmological structures know all about real estate.
We need more boots on the ground zero.
Freebases loaded and four out. Gravity dines at the table of you.
That line drawn in the sand turned out to be stolen from Jack Benny.
A doorknob sits under a sewer grate as though thankful to catch a small break.
The sequel you wrote to Revelations is still out with your agent.
Don't forget to erase the slate.

#SOCIALMEDEA

Kill your darlings quickly in case they are someone else's darlings.
Envy and inferiority are best dealt with through childishly parodic
Twitter accounts.
Who the fuck could possibly care?
Praying feels to me like fumbling with buttons on a shirt tailored for women.
Tranströmer's robots in the skies.
What is up with the trash collectors leaving the crowds behind?
Think of the intimacy lost since we stopped cleaning each other with
our mouths.
Death is a sprinkled donut on a string just out of reach.
Your latest vague statement got me thinking about myself.
Horny fairies know love is true in fairy tails.
Remembering something is actually remembering the last time you
remembered it.
The stone lobbed into the group of soldiers sets them to firing on each other.
Elvis is mainly a figurehead king now.
Sadness's whale needn't come up for air.
Even the rich and famous are still on the hook for blowjobs.
Children are signatures written in blood.
This goddamn jacket is only ten percent George Clooney.
Everyone wants a salacious piece of anguish's latest triumph.
If I only could have held Wisława Szymborska before she died.
All the explodable monuments stand on chairs and hike their skirts.
The time on her face is six minutes to midnight.
Critics are now mostly valves and drains.
It is a time best suited to the voices of mental cases.
A net is just thousands of bridges with no land between.
I'd tap that to the beat of "Wipeout."
Clickbait preceded clicking.
Satan sidelines as the Tooth Fairy for monsters.
Worship pulses its sonar ping into the mind's empty ocean.
One Hundred Years of Solitaire.
I want you all to have as many lols as you can fit in your margins.

The firefight sounds like a string of mistimed firecrackers.
It's almost lunch so please keep posting those hilarious baby Polaroids.
Untrained soldiers are called *people*.
No parking except by permit.
Intelligence is artificial.
All men could be kings if they pissed off the right witches.
City parks with their robot statues and fields of buried teeth and
    maybe-sleeping bodies.
Beware the I'ds of March.
Everyone is welcome to kneel down and watch.
In a minute or so I will probably think of something much more important.
The army withdraws and spills all over your stomach.

#HELTERSKELETOR

Hands are the original necklace.
We each keep mental lists of the heroes we've murdered.
Memo arrives with this week's instructions for anxiety typed in
Comic Sans.
The floors rise up against us as we fall.
Black and white combined now make brown instead of grey.
You suspect your favourite game chirped important info when it knew
you weren't there.
Keep switching channels faster in lieu of changing yourself.
Television's day as mankind's primary source of lighting draws to a close.
Remember that masks worn long enough become faces.
I ache to smash you out of existence.
You say Dumas and I say *dumb ass.*
Each witch's tit flashes its cold peek.
Soon the muscles will dispense with skin.
Things are looking up in the way people do when they've been
knocked to the floor.
Catch the fallout on your tongue.
21 ways to keep your jail cell free of clutter.
Riots are just punk-assed revolts.
The latest piece of laboratory equipment is a ball gag.
Abdomens are the most common sheaths.
What we're ready to call *life* is spreading out.
Sometimes Charlie's angels are just the bugs crawling on Charlie's skin.
Flashing lights are like Heaven on Earth for the bored.
You could spend every moment of the rest of your life watching porn
and never finish.
I would like a planetary topography smooth as the inside of a wedding band.
There will be someone who decides to hate this to rescue prosody.
Schoolgirls mill about in their pens.
Texts flutter in like confetti thrown from a convertible Cadillac.
AM radio keeps its own church.
Look to the ugliest among us for leadership when the world ends.

All is now like watching a stroke happen from inside your own
he@D#$maS*Arj&dHijWz
This is becoming a good day for evil.
Your mother-of-pearl snap buttons are just waiting for you to fuck up.
Brains chew and spew information like black holes.
Eye sockets want to be bullet casings.
That sparkle in your son's eye is just the reflection of an LED.
In the future bondage gear will be formal wear.
Black is the barrel of a gun and white the flash within it.
Tell the children the only way to avoid capture is to stay small or grow
too big for the cuffs.
All the books are already out at the prison library.
The sciences are killing our fetishes.
I have the power.

#GLORYGLORYHOLELLUJA

Anything in Creation can be used as a hammer.
Set poetry down in a storm and watch it become the storm.
Every armchair a valiant steed put out to stud.
My son has started another Instagram account I will have to watch.
What happens in Vegans stays in Vegans.
The children first learn to ransom through tears.
Click every object with your eyes to ensure it's not concealing secret 1ups.
Killers are fairy tales not content to remain unread.
Wearing French cuffs says as much about you as ordering cassis.
Common household pests photobomb moments of microscopic bliss.
Age dampens your need to be always right.
Profile photos allow me to keep up on the narrow missus misses.
There is no traction in memory's mud puddle.
I'd have long since lost a hand to the wheelchair spokes.
What I'd give to once again be unable to distinguish between a human and a marionette.
Cash in your lifetime *likes* for poker chips.
There were the years spent wanting to comb Chewbacca and then this.
God and Disney continue to animate useful objects for fun.
Old folks are champions of moments in the process of being forgotten.
Childhood remains loveseats and ashtrays and a box of Black Magic.
Allot decent time in your schedule for blinking against the light.
Make verse as reliable and rooted as white headstones in a Pentecostal graveyard.
Electrics buzz and crackle like a derby girl's knees.
Young people act as though everything's been leading up to vaping.
Baguette gets slapped down on the counter like a show-off's knobbly cock.
Faith is knowing thought happens even by accident.
Why isn't it tsunami season yet?
I learned to talk just so I could say all this shit.
People mime screaming at other people from inside their cars.
Shame's underwear band folds below age's belly.
Everywhere you look some parents are killing their kids.

Don't dwarf planets sound like they'd have the most darling singing aliens?
A Hindu woman yelling at you is some seriously scary shit.
It's hard to tell whether the scooter or the weight problem came first.
Life is a process of trying to get your consumer data to match your best intentions.
Stats say no one is subscribing to our Lord's Prayer podcast.
Let me know when the phi phenomenon kicks in.
I am just trying to maintain integergrity in an increasingly irrational world.
Blow or bite or wait on the other side.
Punching holes in things is how all the best hammers pray.
The noblesse oblige part will happen when I point but say nothing.

#THEBOOKOFREVOLUTIONS

Be strong and discreet in how you end things.
Enter every room and immediately scout out the emergency exists.
Our tiny reflective robots sprinkle infections over planets we hope to one day shit on.
The most prevalent disability is thought/no thought (circle one).
It's increasingly difficult to not offer a direct assessment.
Lenticular clouds hover as though picking a spot to start their counterstrike.
Every point is terminal in infinity.
Paying dues to people more privileged than you is called *culture*.
You say *I love you* and I say *I love YouTube*.
Seek religiously battery LEDs not flashing red.
The huge bellies and dangly bits of naked old men look dredged from the sea.
Scientists chip away at our constants as effectively as priests shore them up.
No one ever talks about all the goats at the mountain's foot.
Warship is just a misspelling of *worship*.
Schrödinger's babies wriggle under the rubble.
How do you provide a buck and change in an age dedicated to penny nails?
Death continues to be a mostly boom industry.
I was baptized in utero by rum and Marlboros.
Set a circus-worth of zebras end on end and climb the stripes.
Teeth grind down in the face of performed politics.
Irony and parody fucked one night and left us this kid to raise.
You can raise up or you can raze down.
Direct all self-harm into one spot and hope it's not lethal.
If the world had a biography it would be titled *Are You Fucking Kidding Me?*
The difference between a six pack and a small keg is fifteen years and a bad marriage.
My people are only recently mutted.
Who needs art when you got a hatred of women and a selfie of your dick?
The life coaches are tsking.
You now own all the blood I can spare for my enemies.
Photon sails unfold in space like God's hankies.

Fuel lights continue to blink their tyrant orders.
Consciousness is a virus infecting the brain's software.
I wish I didn't have an opinion on the root of our nastiness.
Please consider this slapping you as foreplay.
I made a deal with the Devil that I don't plan to honour.
How easy it would be if the choice was really only red pill or blue pill.
Death the crash and sleep the logout.
Negotiating the point at which I won't bear anymore is more exhausting
    than just bearing.
The emergency is there is no emergency.
Dozing will overtake me the moment I finish typing this line.
Is this thing even on?

Invisible Ink
Published Poems

2002–2019

. . . let go, solo, blast.

THE ARCHITECT

(for LC)

Think this through: every bird
is an architect, her invisible ink pen
circumscribing space, outlining
through-lines, darting her accidental
engineer's eye over each possible
schematic on the blank space of the air;
her quick drive to bank and dive,
roll and glide, drawing isometric
floor plans against the blue,
axonometric site plans, cross sections
where the air reveals elevation
changes necessary for each duct,
pipe, and wire living requires,
the space and narrative demanded
by every swing of door acting
as entrance to, and egress from, the sky.

THE CLEARING

The axe is left between them, stuck in the felled tree,
sun on the handle that sits at an angle like a water pump—

Half-shaded on the veranda she reads children's books
like a censor with an open mind, no agenda but joy—

Over the tree he rubs his knuckles, the skin of his hands
mottled & lumpy as bread with sunflower seeds—

There is a space now between the fence and barn where
she can see him by a culvert, a well, a patch of raspberry—

Even with the tree standing he could see her if he wanted,
stepping around in circles until the branches shaded his eyes.

KITCHEN SINK DRAMA

This is how things get done. It opens
in the kitchen, where all good theatre should,
real at first, necessary at first, until emotion
is lowered like a backdrop on a string.
Then you, crying, then me, staring; telltale
falling against the wall, eyebrows raised
in strange accent, hyperbole and selective
memory making out like horny teenagers
in the dark. This is drama unchained, an ageing
Titan freed from a seaside cliff, a bloody
soliloquy on bent knee, a sword slipping
from a slack hand, the dialogue projected
to an audience wider than just we two here
near the sink; even your most honest
vehemence stage-whispered, even my frown
a painted kabuki. Our mouths active as articulate
puppets, hands blocked so those in the back
rows can follow the pain; this is how it gets done.
Sit down at the table. Breathe. Take your head
from your hands, unlock my lips like a purse.
This is how to do things when you secretly
suspect every word, every sob, every silent
stare is being recorded instead of remembered
only by those involved, or simply forgotten
when the fight ends. As you can see, they are not.

ANIMAL IS MY INNER ANIMAL

You think it too, that you know him.
Have an opinion on his private
mind: aggressive, male, an animal, typical.
Hell, even his own inner voice
says he's all sex, sleep, food, drums,
and pain. But take a step back,
pause and look closely.
Look past the wild red hair,
gripped sticks, and teeth gnashing;
past the twin shows of chasing
skirts and anger; past the hand of The Man
jammed up his ass right to the jaw.
See him in pieces, minutely,
observe how his body stills before
the music starts, how he lags
unfocussed, stares out at the lights
agog; an attack dog calmly
panting on a loose choke chain.
He was led here, brought to this spot
through a strange world of people
who think he's nuts, set down-
stage on a spinning stool,
anchored to the kick drum of his art
to wait for the next song to start.
Watch for that second he takes to himself,
the single beat of calm exposed
by contracting googly iris, by determined
grind of a maw that once hung
open as though in stupid joy.
He lives for this, just like you,
for what clock ticks are left;
not the ones in which he'll roll rim shots
on cue, or play nice with guests,

but those in which his quivering lips
and bugged eyes reveal real
tension, a feral heave in chest and lung,
anticipation of a moment to come
in which he can push every bad impulse
out through constricted pupils,
be unchained at last, let go, solo, blast.

FALSE SPRING

(for RO)

Don't scold the flowers that hold on til the snow,
or the ones that rise too soon when winds go

and the weather psyches us out with scattered
mild days between frozen panes and shattered

petals; they wouldn't listen if they could.
Reaching up is all they know, and all they should.

A NINEVITE PEDAGOGUE RELATES THE LESSON OF JONAH

Sixscore thousand strong then, we heeded,
by royal decree, the words of warning
brought to us from another land—

better safe than smitten, we agreed,
by an undisclosed calamity
sent by a god known for his cleansing

on a terrestrial scale. And, frankly,
it was a nice change from the usual—
a routine, we had recently learned,

of great evil—farming grass and reeds,
vanquishing foes, telling fortunes,
shaping silver and gold and clay tablets

for sale at the market. So we humored
the god and man, fasted from bull
to potter to vizier, tasted nothing, human

and beast united in hunger. Not a touch
of water, not a taste of meat, naught but air
and ululation in our dry mouths.

Black sackcloth was worn widely, tearing
at the soft skin of our noblemen, caressing
the sun-beaten backs of farmers—

and we sat only in the ashes of goats
and sheep and fowl, the meals of forty days
gone up in a jet smoke. And so imagine

our surprise when, at his god's pardon,
the man who saved us with his warning,
fled in anger—taking a sullen

residence east of our city in a hut
meant to provide shelter from the heat
of our summer. Some speculated

that it was his battle for release
from the abdomen of the great fish
that enraged him still—anyone

might harbour resentment after such
an ordeal—others suspected his god
of toying with the shade, driving

the poor fellow mad with heat
at his lookout there on the hill below
our city's glorious rising sun.

But a party sent out to check on his health
returned with the truth—a disturbing
revelation that tumbled us back

to our old ways. We, a people
supposedly unable to tell our left
from right, had been used like an abacus,

a teacher's tool—we were equipment
in an experiment, like the shrivelled gourd
above the prophet and the enormous fish

in whose belly he induced pain and vomitting.

PRIZE PUMPKIN

Cut away all other flowers from the vine,
let one fruit take on mass at the cost
of colour, shape, taste, and all else besides.

A slow spill, it flattens, whatever
pretense of *pumpkin* it began with left
behind in favour of size, every seed

and visceral string within held back
from splitting the pale flesh by simply
adding more skin. It waits in its field,

corpulent shut-in anticipating
the beep of crane reversing in the garden,
its enormous arm telescoping in

through the window's mouth. Ambulance
straps wrap it, cradle it, elevate, evacuate,
bring it to the public. This monumental

shapeless shape is what the blue-ribbon
citation calls *Pumpkin*, and so defined,
it sits in the flatbed on its way to the fair.

NEW REFUGEES WAIT AT THE LIGHTS TO CROSS KENMOUNT ROAD IN A BLIZZARD

The whiteout slid in sideways,
witnessed on the windshield's
editing screen, flickering footage
found the evening news;

the roads wisp, covered in ice but clear
of cars, the traffic lights still
blinking through their little lifetimes:
green, amber, red; again; again.

At the corner huddle five slump-
shouldered forms, waiting for the lights
to change even though there's no
traffic to be seen; sub-Saharan Black

skin and red-rimmed eyes revealed
in patchwork through the escape
hatches parkas make to allow for a face;
wraiths of breath issuing like smoke

from fur-lined chimneys, donated
boots stamping in the vaporous swirl
as if afraid stillness means being
frozen in place. Each one is too new

to say, *Fuck it,* and walk against the light;
too new to not fear offending
a watching by-law or unspoken custom;
too new to know the rule of thumb

here is the same as anywhere:
abandon politeness and law when

the world is trying to kill you,
even a little. Duck, cover, and run

for safety, just like on the news, hoping
the cycle goes a tiny bit slower
each time. Red, amber, green;
again; again. A red hand. A white man.

OLD MAN

(for PL)

News nonetheless arrives because, like wind,
there is always more just behind, pushing in.

We cannot call the death of an old man
sudden or unexpected, but we can

say we were caught unprepared by
him going, and we can once more wonder why.

Today the air again brought its word
like leaves in a gust, blown in from the world

drunk on the very newness of its news:
the same old ending.

This is when windows give all their best views.

A LONG DEAD WOMAN FROM BETHANY IS SADDENED TO SEE LAZARUS SWEPT AWAY

Before he was pulled so suddenly away,
it still amazed her how fated their meeting
seemed—both having lived within

the same lifetime, albeit at alternate ends:
she dying just a year after his birth.
It turned out his family had married into hers

some four generations back, indeed,
many of his livestock were seeded from bulls
and fowl her grandfather had driven

fifteen furlongs in emigration from Jerusalem.
And amid the hazy din in the dark,
heavily populated cave, they spoke of much

they had in common—of the people they knew:
sisters, brothers, nephews, children
of the community now grown and working

at tilling the family land—of their mutual
surprise at the overcrowded nature
of Heaven, or Hell, or wherever this place was

that looked so very much like a crypt
in which a village might bury its parents—
of the wants and needs of the spirit

in a realm without pain, without pleasure,
without water, wind, fire, or even stone—
without a single sensation reminiscent of life

except the panicked impression of gasping
for breath, as though in drowning.
And for four days they strolled

through many caves, some barren and sandy
like their own, others decorated with fine
paints and dyes, still others packed

with tokens and treasures accumulated in life,
but each sealed tight from the air and light
with stones or cubit upon cubit of earth—

tombs packed and fuming with the wet,
vague folk of death, with their raucous talk,
with the footfalls of their wanderings,

with the recollections of their lives or,
in the case of the wispy few so much longer
here, deaths, echoing a muted song

from the damp walls. And to keep him
from dread at the lack of breath,
she listened patiently, spoke softly, kept him

company, wondering all the while how he looked
under the swaddling gravecloths that covered
every feature but the black of his eyes—

knowing that soon enough he would forget
his body, would tire enough of life to remove
the bandages himself, shedding his last

earthly chattel to walk freely
through the stone, out into the light and
dark of a new set of days and a new set of nights.

PRISONER TRANSPORT

There's an exit in back of the courthouse
for those leaving the building but not allowed
to leave. Like fathers away alone—out for now,
but in for good. Two shuffling footsteps
without a roof, then it's back inside, shackles
waiting in the transport—someone's hand
shielding the crown of head, another handcuffing
a thumb-locked comealong for cooperation.
Backing up, warning klaxon, the van idling
in reverse at the walk—waiting for citizens
before tailing into traffic. Listen closely,
Pedestrians. Look past the impassive faces
the Sheriff's officers wear as they hover
in their Kevlar. Stop seeing the crest on each
back door under which some boy,
stupid and brave, has sprayed "Crowbar Motel"
in chunky letters—see instead the slight
change in shadow on the white side panels,
metal buckling in and out rhythmically.
What you're seeing is a sound. Listen.
Hear that weak thumping coming from within?
It's a head pounding against the wall inside.
Maybe it's a cry, maybe a dark deed trying to escape,
but kept in for everyone's good. Muffled beat
from a muscle car woofer pulled up at a red
light—like a pulse of blood, unheard under
the noise of the street. This is how every problem
you are currently mulling sounds to everyone else.

DEATH OF THE DEVOUT CHRISTIAN'S HUSBAND

Someone said today was a perfect Sunday—
the weather, leisure, the possibility,
nothing to spoil this world's flawless scenery.

But, somewhere, an Uncle dies—life's good guy
who clasped and shook little hands so hard they
hurt, each grip a tight reminder of why

growing up both begins and ends painfully.
Everyone's sad, but the Aunt smiles in a way
that seems to say it's all just another day.

Not that it's nothing to lose a love of many
years—but that it is, in the end, customary.
She wasn't worried things were left undone—

she'd read him all the best passages already.

Problematica
New Poems

2013–2020

. . . the answers will vary
depending on who does the asking.

JUST ENJOY THE PARTY, SHE SAID

Did she mean the food?
The drink? The singular decor?
The appearance of the other
guests? Their faces? Small talk?
Where should I stand?
What should I sample? Why
three tables for snacks,
two rooms for coats, no one
organizing the shoes
or answering the door?
Is this a good spot? Why
four reds, open and breathing
on the counter, but only
one white, glassy sides heaving
in gasps, liquid innards
rippled with impact tremors
from dancing in the kitchen?
Why does the stereo bass
escalate in an endless, panic-
inducing Shepard tone
pounding through the floor,
up my leg? Everyone is too close.
I can barely hear anything
except static. Who do I know?
Is she ever coming back?
How did I even get over here?
Everyone is too close. But to what?

GUTTER

The mud has come to life
Along with the first melt;
All water running below the ice
Falls together and melds

Down there in the sewer;
The city's brickwork ewer,

Full of shit and meds,
Black water, grey,
Hair from all our heads,
Fungus, fat, bacterial decay;

Another abyss, into which we spit,
Except when sipping from it.

DOGS

Awake again, the only animal
on the planet that puts on
pants each morning stands,

stretches like any
other that might have been
roused by daylight

instead of crying.
At its feet, another naked
animal also stretches,

flicks an ear, plods off
to piss, leaving the first
to search for its drawers.

When they meet next,
it is in the kitchen over pellet-
filled bowls, news

barking on the radio.
Neither questions who wears
the pants, but one does

peer into the other's eyes
in a way so nearly sentient
that anyone watching

might start to wonder
at what point did each first
begin to think, *I am*.

THINGS CUT IN HALF

Sandwiches, apples, earthworms,
hours by chime, Mars Bars
by knives, date squares, toddlers
by AR-15s, praise, conversations on
uncomfortable topics by glances,
the distance an arrow can fly.
When does a half become whole
again? How far from its other half
must it be in space and time?
They say that if you cut it right,
each half of an earthworm will go on
to become its own full life,
but I don't believe it. Half an apple
needs its other half to look
like a whole anything. Half an hour
can't be whole with both *half*

and *hour* right there in the name.
Half a toddler will never be a whole
again, neither to he who pulled
the trigger nor the one left to drag
her parts away. Like our chat
about your behaviour, where I got to say
only half of what I wanted,
but you think it done. Imagine it
as that date square: if it's cut
behind the counter, set on two plates,
who would know? Or think instead
of the worm, cut by a kid's yellow
safety scissors, or by her teeth
moving though an apple, its half body
twitching while the rest wriggles away,
trying to remember how to be whole.

LATE STORM

An old engine tired of trying
to turn over, gusts,
buffets the siding; wheezing
as if coughing up guts.

The cat wants out, the mice
want in; no one is willing
to accept which side
of the glass they're living on.

Seasons know when to end
when left to themselves;
pressure changes bend
windows, bow the cat's eyes.

Why meddle? Snowflakes reel
on the pane. Map, scar;
palimpsests rewritten, healed,
waiting to mark where you are.

ECTOPIA CORDIS

Luck matters most to those
still beating at fairness's front
door as if expecting an answer.

The year is newer than the snow
but already older than us
asleep here in its incubator;

every day babies line up to press
little omen mouths against
window bars as if waiting to bite

fingers. What an artful junkyard
life is, made by chance
piled in hip-high drifts and cords.

The news says the girl born with a heart
outside her body is in critical condition,
which these days mostly means fine.

WHITE

The snow wasn't white anymore,
nor the milk, nor the moon,
but the night sky was. The poets
too, and their subjects.
Whiter than white, I held
my white feather and asked for
a drink. The bartender was white,
her Russians were white,
and her bra strap was white.
White was the whale
once bled out under the whitecaps,
and white was the elephant
sleeping next to the white mouse.
White the flame, white
the knuckles, the lies, the flags.
White and great was the last hope,
white the deplorable
trash, and white the starched
collars. White was the knight,
his stallion, white, white
his wedding, white the men
in coats closing like a tight defense.
Like white noise. Like white
Christmas. Like white ghosts.
Like white pages (minus the black
ink.) But ghosts aren't white,
nor are pages, nor the lily,
nor the wine, and they never have
been. White went the meat hung
among the white wash, white
went the sheets when asked for
a better explanation of white,
when asked why white never seems
to notice when it's spattered red.

SUMMER FEVER

Fever stinks of timber, an August attic
Under cedar shakes, dripping tar pitch,
Breathing soup, cottonmouth, salted, tasty.

Electric Co. executes its generals,
Styrofoam sags, a Tao of Chemical.
Axonal firing line sits down, lazy.

Open bar, open wound, open-ended
Questions left hanging, the mouth blended,
Teeth upended, lips fibre-dry, pasty.

PICTURE THE AUDACITY OF A PIG

Walking around, huge in all that meat,
uncooked, pressed up against the fence,
daring anything to take a run at it.

Fuck you, is the only phrase a pig
knows, despite the beady intelligence
behind the black eyes swinging

your way. It's done time in the pen
and learned there how to meet a gaze.
It's sick of the slop, tired

of your leavings, looking for the new.
A walking leather jacket filled with meat,
chips on its shoulders where studs

should be, a head without a mohawk
housing more meat, snout made of meat
low to the ground, snuffling about

as if sussing opportunity: vegetable,
mineral, animal, you, me, meat. Kill it
quick, take its meat. Carve out

smaller sections. Follow the antique
dots on the butcher poster hung by a hook
in your kitchen. Cut loin from blade,

ham from hock. Forget its hunger.
Forget that it knows your face. Forget
its eyes. Tiny, dead, watching still.

HOW TO PICK THE PERFECT SAPLING FOR A LEAN-TO

This one. This one is perfect.
Crowded out under the leaves,
it shot straight for the light,
a gap in the crown-shy trees,
taking off, stretched and narrow,
a featherless arrow aimed high.
Resolute, it spent itself entirely
on growing taller, no consideration
but ambition for the gold above,
regardless how slim a trunk
is left behind. This one wanted
the light and light it got.
Light lured it from its roots.
Light urged it up. Light implored it
to spread its green hands
against the blue, to look back
down like a father glancing over
his shoulder at the road
by which he came, the road
he took away from all things
familiar. A lesson is here:
see how hard it tried to survive?
To win? Even so, the same
rains that helped it grow now
soak its leaves, draw its arc
down from the light above
back to us here among the weeds.

SWEAR JAR

Coins clink while falling
into the jar on the dresser,
a few more paid out

each night, clothes doffed
as the day exchanges its tallied
frustrations for quiet

dreams of what might be
saved up. Meanwhile,
hours are spent in quarters

fished from the meagre
bank time granted us each
at birth, never to be replaced,

not even a single penny.
Life begins this way: penitent,
full, flush with change

and chance, then loses
its metal pieces one by one
until the jar is transparent again.

It seems forever is forever
nickel-and-diming us, no matter
what the fuck the cost.

GRACE

The first graceful ape is long
since lost, her brow bone
unfossilized, ground back down

to soil: feeding the grasslands
that feed the herds that feed hers.
Her record is incomplete,

no illustration of her remains,
curvy spine, splayed pelvis,
no cast of a print recovered

from the riverbed clay, no account
in pigment on stone of how
she pointed and named a star.

Everything important has been
taken by time, as things tend to be.
What's left behind is the same,

always right here in this line:
grace, and the chance to see it
in you, in me, in what's between.

STORM DOOR

Every ray of light slants,
a staircase leading to its own
ground level exit.

Out front the snow falls,
soft as dust from a saw buried
in a carpenter's pencilled line.

What looks like disorder
almost always has its own order,
the only rules are: no rules.

This is what gives chance
the chance to shine, over time.
A shirt falls from its hook

behind the door, knocks
its buttons on the wooden floor,
waits for an answer.

THE PERSEIDS

Light shoots from his pinprick
eyes in an array, surprise
lines around a cartoon hero's head.

Off balance, back on his heels
with brows high as surprised stars,
he leans into Andromeda,

cocks his ear up towards Cassiopeia,
listening to lascivious whispers;
dirty plans they'd unleash on him

if he'd just leave the other
woman's many-fanged head
in his own sky. All night lights fire

from his pupils, his asterism
behind the truth falling earthward.
What could come from beyond

a conquering hero? Nothing
is as sexy to us as gods:
those who live above the heroes

who live above us, and who always
look down on everything we do.
They're like supervillains,

leaning from one panel to the next,
getting off on their ridiculous
plans to one day destroy the world.

IN SEASON

Sun will soon be widely available
again, like bellybuttons in the '90s,
warm and untouchable.

Do not look directly at the tummy
next to you at the fruit rack;
it looks back and is only trouble.

Stare instead at the orange stems,
cyclopean green eyes in each glowing
face, pocked skin puckering

to a point, curved rinds of spacetime
collapsing in on themselves, crushing
to blackness, a universal umbilicus.

Always make the safest bet
with your eyes by looking at only
the most compact stars;

because light wants to be dark,
and darkness wants to become light
by pulling everything,
                                        including itself, down.

LOT'S EURYDICE

The world changed as I stared
it right in the face, absently
humming the song that got me

here. Like a wife drawn
out of her old world and ageing
into a new beauty despite her

best intentions, nothing
looked different until I looked
back while walking away.

Soon, I'll get a set of new
nows, but will only ever
want a single then,

that one tick of the clock
in which she too risked it all
to look back at me tagging along.

I was in tune. I was strong
and I was tall. A pillar not yet gone
to dust. Like I remember myself.

SPECIAL WEATHER STATEMENT

Red sky that morning was an alarm
ringing the way an oven
element glows under its kettle,

teapot tempest raging nearby;
shit lined itself up facing the proverbial
fan at an angle of greatest effect;

the frying pan held its nose, jumped
into the fire; cats and dogs
fell in buckets like balloonists

without balloons; the parade
was long since soaking wet; no one
could break the ice; no one had

the foggiest; they were all under
the weather. Winged pigs
learned quickly which way the wind

was blowing; heatwaves
crashed on life's beaches;
the sea was as pure

as the driven slush; those
on Cloud Nine had lost their heads
in Clouds Ten through Fifteen;

the mail continued to arrive,
a windfall, regardless.
Fair-weather fiends swooped

upwards in the storm, loose
papers on fire catching
the drift; we all danced

for rain checks; wind of what
was coming arrived
and ruined the surprise;

thunder was found in the lockup
where it had been set aside as
evidence in the theft trial to come.

Things had been breezy until
we threw caution like doves
to the wind; the sky had taken

its left turn veering away from right
as rain, darkening over every
last ray of hope. We were full

windbags, like tuneless pipes
just starting to blow; we were on
thin ice; had failed to notice

the red sky last night; the calm
had come and gone before
the something something;

somewhere the rainbow chasing
was over itself. And even as
it was ending, even when we were

being taken by storm, we were
only beginning to realize
how difficult it would be for anyone

to find their place in the sun
by the shine of a moon
gone blue from holding its breath.

There was no doubt about it,
in the cold light of day it was pretty
much likely we'd finally blown it.

NESTING INSTINCT

The cat crawls away to find its place
to die, as will I, in my own time.
Her face peels back from its skull and eyes
as she decays in the attic, lost
to all who knew her soft touch, alone
at last.
          The remains she leaves behind,
fur and bones in a draft-ridden roost,
like something balled and thrown and pursued,
reminds whoever finds them up there
in the winter rafters of what was
owned, lost, a looked-for, but forgotten
hereafter.
               One nest in which she's born,
another for dying. And between,
revising many times, she attempts
to perfect a spot in which to lie,
like me with this line, turned first by tongue,
then on the page, then left here for you
                                                            to find.

INCERTAE SEDIS

Belonging is mostly longing
because, like all weirdos, wishes
don't know where to go.

It's a tired reply to an old
judgment: fine, cut the baby in half.
At the party an awkward doctor

stands alone near the table
where a melon has been chopped
into wedges despite

the melon baller left right
there beside the subcutaneous
prosciutto. Like the man,

nothing here seems to connect
with anything else. So, let's leave it
to sit quietly tucked away

for years, disorganized, unused,
undescribed, another odd single-
purpose tool in a kitchen

junk drawer, or footnotes on
a taxonomic paper, until its use
becomes clear. The question

forever remains: *What belongs
here?* but answers will typically vary,
depending on who is asking.

IRISH EXIT

Make a memorable entrance,
hum along, but leave with circumspect
grace; this is how I work to walk
into, and stumble out of, every place.

Eleven, midnight, last call; the exits
all scoped out on entry, escape routes
planned past extended hands,
around the bottles, down the hall.

Even now, from this corner I see
the party starting to flag, the guests
looking tired as sloppy kisses flow,
and I dissolve away like ashes

in the dregs. I despise long goodbyes,
the hugs they risk, the just-one-more-things
to say; better to be dead and gone long
before the fat lady opens her mouth to sing.

FLUTE LESSON

It used to be we scoffed at flautists,
those whose decline began with Wolfgang
and ended abruptly at Jethro Tull.

What use is a flautist, much less a flute?
What do they do besides give
little birds flight in Prokofiev?

The rolled eyes have it: flutes bore,
and flautists are *whack*, which to young
folk back then meant, *ineffably negative*.

But here I am now, older and lying
awake, worried for the flautists:
How can they fly? What if the birds go?

HITCHER

What I want is for God to show up
recognizably, in a form I can process
and accept—a brown '75 Nova
with tan Naugahyde bench seats.
He'd pull up and open the door,
saying, *Hop in, kid,* and we'd head off
west without seatbelts,
matching the speed of all the other cars
going our way. And when I grew
tired of thanking Him for stopping,
I'd stretch out on the hot back seat
like I was a child again—watching
the telephone poles pass with hypnotic
regularity until it grew dark
from evening or my eyes closing.
And I'd lose track of time, and I'd lose
track of space, and I'd wake
in the night to the V8 rumble and the last
streetlamps disappearing behind Us.

THE VERGE
(for DS)

Everywhere, the verge;
just before or after
everywhere as well.
Green edge, black edge;
merge. Moments
moments before becoming
seconds, but already split
seconds before the surge.

YOU CAN'T SAY ANYTHING ANYMORE

The laundry is airing on the line—
now it's everyone's problem,
especially downwind.

Silence shapes decision,
and decision the order of things
hung out to dry.

Some stains really pop after
a good shake—love's and hate's
crusted amoebas in yellows

and reds, rising from white
rugs hung over the fence,
sheets clipped tight

to the line, lace panties
waving from single pegs.
Inhale as though about to speak.

There they are—blemishes—plain
as the nose you use to test
the air. The wind whips them

into white-flag-blurs, and while
you logically know marks remain,
if they wait long enough,

the stains themselves know
that sooner or later you'll forget, move
on—see, smell, and know nothing.

PLACES, EVERYONE

It is late, and you are always late
arriving, and the bell has rung
and the lobby lights are flashing—
so, watch the crowd to see
where you're supposed to go.
Track the shapes of those ahead
looking to find a seat, filing
through the dark beyond the doors,
but stopping before the curtains.
It was a mad rush getting here,
but now it's out of your hands,
and soon the spotlights will rise
with everyone in their proper
places and the tale will be told.
It is time to make your last
breath deep enough to recount
how all went in its entirety,
the story of how you came to be
standing here in line at the will-call,
late and waiting on a ticket
reserved in your name for a show
you aren't even sure is still running,
and of which you heard only one thing—
there will be no intermission.

Acknowledgements

Thanks to: Elisabeth de Mariaffi, my first reader and true love; Mark Callanan, my advisor, confidante, and pal; my other readers and editors for the new poems in this book, including Andreae Callanan, Liz Howard, Jacob McArthur Mooney, Sina Queyras, Carmine Starnino, Paul Vermeersch, Claire Wilkshire; and to my editor, Michael Holmes, who has held, since about 1993, the following roles in my life: crush, teacher, hero, drinking buddy, Devil's Advocate, enabler, wisdom dispenser, editor, publisher, friend, and brother. Extra thanks are also due to Adam Sol, whose foolish mind I admire.

Many of the poems collected here first appeared in the following papers, arts magazines, and journals, so please support them by buying subscriptions where possible: *Alphabet City*, the *Antigonish Review*, *Backwards City Review*, *BafterC*, *Canadian Poetries*, *Capilano Review*, *Contemporary Verse 2*, *Danforth Review*, *Descant*, *Drunken Boat*, *Echolocation*, *Event*, *Exile*, *Fiddlehead*, *Geist*, *Globe & Mail*, *Grain*, *Granta*, *Hazlitt*, *Iowa Review*, *Jacket*, *LaPetiteZine*, *Lemon Hound*, *Literary Review of Canada*, *London Magazine*, *Maisonneuve*, *Mid-American Review*, *New American Writing*, *New Quarterly*, *New Welsh Review*, *Nth Position*, *Ontario Review*, *Orlando Sentinel*, *Painted Bride Quarterly*, *Pasture*, *Pequod*, *Prairie Fire*, the *Prairie Journal of Canadian Literature*, *PRISM International*, the *Puritan*, *Radical Society*, *Rampike*, *Riddle Fence*, *Slope*, *Taddle Creek*, and the *Walrus*.

Poems in the Invisible Ink section of this book were published in journals, but never republished as part of a collection like many of the others. Chronologically, they are:

"A Long Dead Woman from Bethany is Saddened to See Lazarus Swept Away" (*Iowa Review*, 2002)
"A Ninevite Pedagogue Relates the Lesson of Jonah" (*Pequod*, 2002)
"The Clearing" (*Echolocation*, 2003)
"Kitchen Sink Drama" (*Contemporary Verse* 2, 2007)
"Death of a Devout Christian's Husband" (*Riddle Fence*, 2013)
"Prisoner Transport" (*Riddle Fence*, 2014)
"New Refugees Wait at the Lights to Cross Kenmount Road in a Blizzard" (*Contemporary Verse* 2, 2016)
"Animal Is My Inner Animal" (The *Walrus*, 2017)
"Prize Pumpkin" (*NewPoetry*, 2017)
"The Architect," "False Spring," "Old Man," (*Riddle Fence*, 2019)

Over the years, many of the poems herein have been featured in anthologies, including: *Introductions: Poets Present Poets* (Fizthenry Whiteside), *The IV Lounge Reader* (Insomniac Press), *Poetry After 9-11: An Anthology of New York Poets* (Melville House), *100 Poets Against the War* (Salt), *Das Gedächtnis der Wörter* (Alexander Verlag Berlin), *Breathing Fire 2* (Nightwood), *The New Canon* (Véhicule Press), *Gertrude Stein Award Anthology* (Green Integer Press), *Jailbreaks & Re-creations* (Biblioasis), *Open Wide a Wilderness* (Wilfred Laurier Press), *Alhambra International Poetry Calander* (Alhambra, 2009, 2010, 2011), and *Best Canadian Poetry*. Thanks to the editors of these publications.

In 2005, a small number of sonnets that would appear in *The Rush to Here* were published with the title *A Deadly Set of Negotiations* (a letterpress edition) by Frog Hollow Press. In 2010, a small hardcover edition of selected poems called *Exit Strategy* appeared in New Zealand with Kilmog Press.

During the last twenty-five years of writing, I have received grants and prizes that have allowed me to concentrate on writing the work presented here. Thanks to the Canada Council for the Arts, The Ontario Arts Council, The Toronto Arts Council, ArtsNL, and the City of St. John's for their investment and support.

About the Author

George Murray has taught or lectured on poetry at New School University, The New York Times Knowledge Network, Princeton, University of British Columbia, University of Toronto, Memorial University, and York University, among others. He is the editor of Bookninja.com and NewPoetry.ca, has been a contributing editor at *Canadian Notes & Queries*, the *Drunken Boat*, *Literary Review of Canada*, and *Maisonneuve Magazine*, and has served as St. John's Poet Laureate (2013–2017). He grew up in rural Ontario, and has previously lived in Toronto, rural Italy, and New York City, but since 2006, has called St. John's, Newfoundland his home.

Permissions

Thank you to Jared Bland for facilitating permission to reprint originally collected in the McClelland & Stewart Collections *The Cottage Builder's Letter* and *The Hunter*.

"Automatic Doors" by George Murray from *The Rush to Here*, Nightwood Editions, 2007, www.nightwoodeditions.com

"Days of Glass" by George Murray from *The Rush to Here*, Nightwood Editions, 2007, www.nightwoodeditions.com

"Ditch" by George Murray from *The Rush to Here*, Nightwood Editions, 2007, www.nightwoodeditions.com

"Drawing in Water" by George Murray from *The Rush to Here*, Nightwood Editions, 2007, www.nightwoodeditions.com

"Exit Strategy" by George Murray from *The Rush to Here*, Nightwood Editions, 2007, www.nightwoodeditions.com

"Go" by George Murray from *The Rush to Here*, Nightwood Editions, 2007, www.nightwoodeditions.com

"Many Worlds" by George Murray from *The Rush to Here*, Nightwood Editions, 2007, www.nightwoodeditions.com

"Mostly the World Waits" by George Murray from *The Rush to Here*, Nightwood Editions, 2007, www.nightwoodeditions.com

"Rearview Mirror" by George Murray from *The Rush to Here*, Nightwood Editions, 2007, www.nightwoodeditions.com

"Rush" by George Murray from *The Rush to Here*, Nightwood Editions, 2007, www.nightwoodeditions.com

"Silence Is a Dead Language" by George Murray from *The Rush to Here*, Nightwood Editions, 2007, www.nightwoodeditions.com

"The Devil" by George Murray from *The Rush to Here*, Nightwood Editions, 2007, www.nightwoodeditions.com

"The Unequal Gaze" by George Murray from *The Rush to Here*, Nightwood Editions, 2007, www.nightwoodeditions.com

"This is Not Your Story" by George Murray from *The Rush to Here*, Nightwood Editions, 2007, www.nightwoodeditions.com

"Truck Stop Gothic" by George Murray from *The Rush to Here*, Nightwood Editions, 2007, www.nightwoodeditions.com

"War Memorial" by George Murray from *The Rush to Here*, Nightwood Editions, 2007, www.nightwoodeditions.com